marie claire
Maison

Living with
COLOR

Discover your personal palette

marie claire
Maison

Living with
COLOR
Discover your personal palette

Bridget Bodoano

This edition first published in 2008 by
Quadrille Publishing

Editorial director: **Jane O'Shea**
Creative director: **Helen Lewis**
Editor and project manager: **Anne McDowall**
Art direction and design: **Lucy Gowans**
Production: **Vincent Smith, Bridget Fish**

ISBN: 978 184400 638 0
Printed in China

Library of Congress Cataloging-in-Publication Data
Bodoano, Bridget.
Living with color : discover your personal palette
with examples from
Marie Claire maison / Bridget Bodoano.
p. cm.
Includes index.
ISBN 978-1-84400-638-0 (pbk.)
1. Color in interior decoration. I. Marie Claire
maison. II. Title.
NK2115.5.C6B63 2008
747'.94--dc22

2008021725

Contents

Introduction 6

Color Effects 10

White Light 24

White Plus 36

Glorious Technicolor 66

Historical Associations 86

Rich Tapestry 104

Pale and Interesting 124

Watercolor Technique 142

Useful Addresses 154

Index 158

Picture Credits 160

Color is all around us in various forms. Nature gives us the brilliance of sky blue, grass green, and poppy red but also the less definable, subtle colorings of a pink dawn, pebble grays, and lichen greens. Away from the natural world, we are faced with a plethora of beautiful and varied colors in everything from clothing to building materials, and when it comes to interiors, the range of colors now available is huge, not only in paint, wallpaper, and textiles, but also in flooring, furniture, and accessories. Being presented with such a wide choice may be wonderful, but unless we have very definite ideas, choosing a paint color for the walls can easily turn into a daunting rather than a pleasurable experience.

We all respond to color in different ways, but our choice of colors for our home will be influenced by several factors, including not only our personal taste but also current fashions, the architectural style of our home, and how we live in it. Color has a huge impact on an interior and we can use it to make a

Previous page:
The palette of colors in this room has been deliberately restricted so as not to detract from or compete with the landscape outside, which provides its own ever-changing, glorious color scheme.

Opposite: *This shocking pink extravaganza is not for the faint-hearted, but, in fact, keeping everything in the room one color can create a harmonious and surprisingly restful atmosphere.*

space feel cooler or warmer, larger or smaller, lighter or darker. But color also has an effect on our emotions and we can use it to create an ambience to suit different moods. Bright colors are normally associated with energy and stimulation, while the paler, more neutral tones are thought to be more relaxing.

Just as there are fashions in clothes, interiors are subject to trends, and if you love the latest clothes, you probably also want your home to reflect your fashion credibility. But in the same way that the latest colors are not always the most flattering to our skin tones or hair color, the latest vogue for interiors may not be the most suitable for you and your home. In addition, unlike with clothes, color in the home is all around us, and most of us decorate to last for years rather than months—a good reason for any interior scheme to include a few timeless classics.

Your response to color is a highly personal thing. Often the best and most interesting homes are those that reflect the personalities and passions of their owners, so don't be afraid to follow your instincts and give in to your emotions when it comes to choosing a color scheme—it can have a direct effect on your well-being and will certainly make using color in your home a more rewarding and enjoyable experience.

1

COLOR EFFECTS

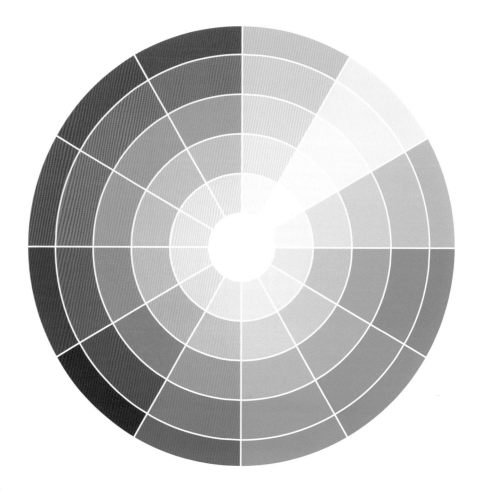

The Full Spectrum

Color is a complex subject that has fascinated scientists and artists for many hundreds of years. While it is not necessary to fully understand the science of color, it is useful to have an awareness of how colors are formed.

There are three pure or "primary" colors: red, blue, and yellow. Along with black and white, these colors can, in theory, be used to create all other colors. The strength and general appearance of colors will depend on many factors, including the source of the color itself, the medium or material, and methods of manufacture. Over centuries, the introduction of new ingredients and techniques in the dyeing and printing processes has widened the scope of color, and today's advances in science and material technology, including computer-generated images, means that many more variations, versions, and intensities of colors are now available.

When exploring color theory, it can be helpful to view colors within a color wheel. Here you can see how the gradual adding of one primary to another changes red to orange to yellow, takes yellow through green to blue, and transforms blue into violet and then red. Colors containing red and yellow are generally accepted to be warm, while colors near blue are cooler.

Opposite: *This room appears as a joyful celebration of color. The large space and pale-colored walls and floor allow the very strong colors used for the furnishings, pictures, and paper lanterns to make an impact.*

COLORFUL LANGUAGE

The language used to describe color is rich and varied and has occupied the pen and imagination of poets and writers for centuries. While there is a tendency toward the fanciful in the decorating business, the names given to colors can be useful, especially on color charts, where a name can provide valuable clues as to the content, provenance, characteristics, and mood of a particular color. Descriptions may also include references to landscape, plants, and wildlife as well as helpful words such as fresh, cool, calm, or spicy. However, with so many colors now available, not all the names are perhaps quite so informative.

COLORFUL TERMS

- **Hue**—color
- **Tint**—color with white added
- **Shade**—color with black added
- **Tone**—color with gray added
- **Monochromatic**—containing shades, tones, and tints of only one color
- **Achromatic**—no color, just white, black, and gray

These descriptions are not always used in their strictly correct manner, but it is generally accepted that "shade" refers to variations of one color and "tones" to the strength or character. "Tint" is commonly used to denote a small amount or hint of one color in another.

The Effect of Color

Colors vary according to their context and the quality and amount of light that falls on them, so it is not surprising that they, in turn, have an effect on their surroundings. Some of those effects are described here.

If there is one lesson to be learned about decorating with color it is that you should always try out colors in a room before deciding on which one to use. Fortunately, these days many paint manufacturers sell trial sizes, which enable you to paint a large enough sample to be able to fully appreciate its impact. Wallpaper retailers will often cut a sizeable piece for you to try, and while stores may not be keen to supply a large sample of fabric, they will normally allow you to buy a small quantity. It really is worth spending some money on getting it right as mistakes can be expensive.

Color on color
Colors play tricks on the eye. The "flicking" effect that occurs when you place bright red and bright green next to one another demonstrates how powerful the effect of one color on another can be. Indeed, colors change depending on the color they are next to. For example, orange on a red background will look yellow but orange on yellow will seem red. On green, it will appear as an even darker red but on violet it becomes more yellow. Colors will show up well against white, while on a black, indigo, or purple background they can appear even more intense.

Taking the temperature
Reds and yellows tend to have a warming effect on an environment whereas blues and greens visually lower the temperature. The degree of warmth in a color can be adjusted by mixing warm colors into cool ones and vice versa so that it is possible to have warm greens and blues and cool yellows. However, light and the other colors and materials used in a room can also visually warm or cool the atmosphere. Wood and textiles are good at warming while silvery metal and glass are effective coolants.

Sizing it up
Color can have a dramatic effect on the size—or apparent size—of a room. On the whole, dark colors make a space feel smaller, while light colors will make it look larger, particularly if a single pale color is used on everything, including walls, paintwork, floors, and furnishings. A dark-colored floor will make a room look smaller as will a brightly painted or papered wall or dark paintwork. Whether this matters and affects your choice of color will depend on personal preference and the size of your space. Although the "light and airy" feel is very much in vogue, a deep color can be used even in a small room to make it feel warmer and more cozy, or just more fun.

Around the clock
Colors also change their appearance at different times of the day. This change can be quite dramatic and a color that you love by day can become too warm, cold, dark, or ineffectual in artificial light. For example, red looks darker at night whereas blue looks lighter. However, it can work the other way and colors that seem too heavy in the day can be dramatic and sexy at night.

Light show
White reflects light and black absorbs it, so it goes without saying that a

Right: *The power of color to change the mood is well demonstrated here, where the same space appears in different guises from dark and mysterious through cool and energizing to warm and sunny. The colors of the accessories have also been changed to enhance the effect.*

white room will feel and look bright and need less lighting than a dark one. However, the light-absorbing properties of colors are not always immediately obvious and some pale colors can be surprisingly difficult to illuminate. This is most noticeable with some paints and is partly due to the light-reacting properties of the constituents in the paint. This is particularly true of "historical" paints, especially if they are manufactured according to traditional recipes, which not only contain more pigment but also have a gray base rather than the comparatively bright white base of modern paints.

Compass points

Rooms facing north or northeast generally appear cooler, and a color that looks bright in a south- or southwest-facing room may look disappointingly dull in a sun-starved environment. For this reason, especially if you are using white, go for a warmer tone in cool rooms and keep the cooler shades for the sunny environments. And if you are using an intense color in two rooms that face different directions, you may find you need to go one or even two shades darker to achieve the same effect in the north-facing space.

Seasonal effect

Just like the seasons, colors change their appearance throughout the year, and those that look fresh and bright in summer can turn cold and unfriendly in winter when harsher light, shorter days and lack of leaves change the ambience. This can be very noticeable in a room painted white, where the onset of colder weather may well change a fresh and bright room into one that is chilly and unwelcoming. In the same way, colors that warm up an interior during winter months may feel oppressive and too intrusive on hot sunny days.

Left: *A bathroom is a good place to experiment with dark colors—they will contrast beautifully with white fittings and will therefore be prevented from looking too oppressive.*

Opposite: *Gray can be a cold, forbidding color, especially when used for walls and furniture, but in this interior, the two slabs of bright color and the mellow tones of the wooden floor help to create a warm ambience.*

Crossing continents

While traveling abroad, it is easy for us to be inspired by colors and to be tempted to try to incorporate them into our homes. However, colors that look good in one country may not work well in another where the light conditions and landscape are different. Deep, bright blue looks wonderful in Morocco or Greece but dark and forbidding in northern Europe. Terra-cotta and creamy orange shades, which are great in Tuscany, take on a muddy hue in northerly climes. Conversely, pale yet subtle colors appear sophisticated in cool climates but suffer from the bleaching effect of bright sunlight.

Casting shadows

Different surface treatments and textures will also affect the appearance of colors. A smooth gloss paint will reflect light and therefore look lighter than the same shade in a matte finish. A flat piece of fabric will look darker when it is made up into drapes because the folds cast shadows, and similarly, a textured carpet can look darker when laid than it did in a small sample. Architectural features such as decorative moldings and ceiling roses are subject to the same shadow effects, so if you want them to look the same color as the walls and ceiling, paint them a shade lighter.

The Psychology of Color

We all have our own response to color: one person's gorgeous pink is another's sugary horror, and while some people think of red as energizing and stimulating, others find it overpowering and even sinister. Many people believe that color can exert a powerful psychological effect on our bodies and emotions and there is much evidence to back this up. Individuals often employ color specialists to help choose clothes and interiors to suit their personality but professional color consultants are also employed to ensure that public buildings, hospitals, and offices provide an appropriate ambience, be it stimulating, soothing, or even authoritative.

The psychology of color is a fascinating topic but you don't need to study it in depth in order to find out what colors suit you. Trust your own instinct and don't be afraid to act on your initial response to a color; after all, your brain and subconscious have a lifetime of research for you to draw on!

Although our response to color is a very personal thing, however, there are certain generally accepted ideas regarding the character, effects, and associations of different colors, some of which are shown opposite.

Left: *This green room, with chair and table painted to match the walls, looks clean, fresh, and cheerful. The pretty printed cushions and rug add extra warmth and comfort.*

Red stimulating, hot, passionate, menacing, dangerous

Yellow warm, sunny, bright, happy, mellow, sickly

Blue cool, pure, clean, cold, melancholic, oppressive

Orange cheerful, warm, zingy, dominant

Green calm, natural, fresh, restorative, cold

Purple rich, sophisticated, spiritual, somber, cheap

Pink soft, soothing, feminine, romantic, fun, sugary, sickly

Gold expensive, prestigious, mellow, decorative, brash

Silver cool, sharp, sophisticated, functional, cold

White pure, clean, light, cold

Black dramatic, elegant, sophisticated, depressing, sinister

Creating a Palette

We live in a fast-paced world and when we are decorating and improving our homes, we are often impatient to get it all done quickly. However, rushing the process sometimes leads to the wrong decisions being made on colors and furnishings and these mistakes can prove costly. It might be worth following the advice given in a book on interior decorating written in 1926: "Never try to choose anything connected with the decoration of your house if you are tired. You must be able to concentrate and you cannot if you are fatigued. Don't try to choose too many things on one day as the senses become numbed and one loses one's judgment. Be lazy about it and slow in settling."

INSPIRATION

If you find the idea of putting together a color palette a daunting one, don't be shy about taking ideas from those who are very good at it. The palettes used by great artists and designers are freely available through postcards, books, magazines, and exhibitions as well as stores, movies, and TV. If you like bright colors, take a look at the work of Matisse; if you prefer subtlety, look at the way color was used in 18th-century houses; if you adore retro, study your favorite style in more detail; and if you are a fashion junkie, then take your color lead from your favorite designers.

Don't rely simply on small samples of paint colors and fabrics—you will be unable to see how the colors react with one another. Colors look different against a white background, so when you are using paint charts, it's wise to cut out the color swatch so that you can see how it works next to other colors. Try to use as large an area of color as possible and make good use of trial-size pots of paint. Always take samples with you and try to make decisions at home—the lighting in stores makes colors look quite different from the way they will appear in a domestic environment.

When planning your color scheme it is a good idea—and good fun—to gather together a collection of items containing not only colors swatches, textiles, and flooring samples, but also postcards, fruit and vegetables, objects that will be in the room, and favorite possessions—in fact anything that represents not only the colors but also the ambience you want to achieve.

PLANNING FOR COLOR USE

When you are making decisions on color, you will need to think about how the space will be used, by whom and when as well as taking into account the size and location of the room.

When do you use the room?
Wild colors and adventurous color schemes may be great for a bathroom or small living room but for living areas in regular use it may be wise to tone things down a bit.

Who uses it?
If you share your home with others, don't forget to take their likes and dislikes into consideration.

What do you do in it?
Stimulating colors in a bedroom may keep you awake and in a living room may stop you from relaxing, but they could make you work better in a study and feel more cheerful slaving over a hot stove in the kitchen.

Opposite: Paintings provide perfect palettes for an interior color scheme. Here the colors of the wall and floor are taken directly from this wonderfully exuberant painting while still allowing it to be the center of attention.

THE ART OF COLOR SCHEMING

Here are a few painterly tips for you to consider before taking the final decisions on your color palette.

- **Landscape**
Take into consideration other colors around you—it may be the backyard or view outside the window, or the color of the walls in the neighboring room.

- **Architecture**
Take into account the style of the building—some colors suit some buildings better than others.

- **Portrait**
Include a picture of yourself with all your samples—it sounds mad but you should be able to see if you look comfortable in your proposed color scheme.

- **Still life**
Take all your palette ingredients and make a still life in the room to be decorated so that you can see how everything reacts with each other in those particular surroundings.

- **Abstract**
Don't confine yourself to paint and fabrics—a pair of striped woolly gloves or a bowl of blueberries and yogurt could be the basis for a color scheme.

light

bright

brilliant

shine

snow

ice

WHITE LIGHT

crisp white cotton

freshly laundered linen

white chocolate

light cream

smooth white pebbles

It may be a cliché, but there's no denying that white makes things appear lighter and feel bigger, and for that reason it is an obvious decorating choice. If you are unsure what to do in your home and the old decor is hampering your thought processes, a coat of white will certainly clear the palette. Unfortunately, white is often seen as the easy option, a good solution when decisiveness and inspiration fail. But while plenty of white paint can undoubtedly be a panacea for the ills of a gloomy, tired interior, it really works best when it is a used as a definite statement. You should give as much thought to a white interior as you would to a more complex color scheme.

A dark and dingy space can certainly be transformed with a lick of white paint into a much more pleasant environment, but white can also create an atmosphere that is cold, soulless, and uninviting. The success of a white interior depends on using the right white and your choice should take into account the quality of light and the architecture of your space as well as the colors and finishes on floors, fittings, and furnishings. Nowadays there is a wide (and rather confusing) selection of whites to choose from. Many of the old "historic" whites are not white at all but this still leaves plenty that are and they fall roughly into cool and warm categories depending on what other colors they contain.

Because of its ubiquity and low price, "brilliant white" is a popular choice. However, it is not easy to use: this bright white contains blue and therefore tends to be cold and a little harsh. It is likely to sharpen objects and will highlight anything that is inferior in design or quality, or is grubby or damaged.

Often it is better to go for warm whites, which have very small amounts of red, yellow, and brown added to create a gentler tone that softens edges, is kinder to furnishings and the eye, and creates a more restful ambience. Whites with a greenish tinge are known to be relaxing but they can look cold and clinical—more hospital than hospitable. However, some of the "historic" whites contain more muted green undertones that are warmer and will work well in both old and new properties.

Opposite: *The use of white unifies the contrasting styles of the beautifully detailed paneling and the modern furniture in this room, creating an impression of simple elegance.*

White Out

The white box filled with white objects may have become a design cliché and therefore slightly unfashionable, but it can nevertheless look stunning, and for purist, disciplined minimalists, it is still the only color of choice. Of course, you don't have to be a dedicated modernist or minimalist to make the all-white interior work well—though it does help if your virtues include tidiness and cleanliness. Few would disagree that white is perfect in spaces where the architecture is the main attraction because it will not detract from the design, but it can also be used in more prosaic surroundings where it will do the opposite and play down inadequacies, drawing attention away from unattractive features.

"White out" means not only white walls but also white furniture, fittings, and accessories, white bed linen, cushions, and upholstery, lampshades, shades, china, vases, bathroom fittings, and tiles. If you want to go all the way, a white floor will complete the picture, increasing the feeling of light and space. In fact, a white floor is not as impractical as it sounds: white ceramic tiles, floor paint, vinyl, or painted wooden boards are all hardwearing, easy-to-clean surfaces, and unless you have pets and children providing a constant supply of footprints and spills, a white floor is easy to look after. Even if you think white would be impractical for large areas of floor, you could try it in a bathroom or small kitchen.

It is easy to get carried away with the all-white theme and you can end up spoiling the effect by overaccessorizing. Try to resist the temptation to fill the space with white objects. You don't need to purify your home by throwing out anything colored, just keep these things out of sight.

WAYS WITH WHITE

There are a number of ways in which you can use an all-white scheme, depending on the style of your home, your personal taste, and the state of your bank balance.

Classy white out
This is the ultimate white experience, created with smooth, blemish-free surfaces, high-quality materials and finishes—think of white polished stone floors, modern minimalist furniture in acrylics, and leather with shiny metal detailing. If a softer, more traditional style is your preference, however, you can opt instead for white painted bespoke wooden furniture and fittings with lots of white textiles.

Functional white-out
If your style aspirations exceed your surroundings and you lack the cash to bring it up to scratch, a covering of white paint will help to disguise shortcomings of furniture or surfaces and create a fashionable industrial or workshop feel. Rough walls, floorboards, old fittings, exposed brickwork, and pipework all respond well to a coat of white.

Thrifty white out
If you tend to furnish your house from yard sales and flea markets, why not try unifying everything with copious amounts of white paint and fabric. Paint walls, woodwork, floorboards, wooden shelves and fittings, and furniture—even nasty stuff can look good under a generous coating of white eggshell or gloss paint—and dress the room with white drapes, winow shades, bed linen, and lampshades to complete the look.

Economy white out

When it comes to buying inexpensive furniture, the safest color choice is often white as the alternatives are usually veneers (which can look cheap and can be difficult to match up with other veneers), primary colors, or colors that frankly look cheap. However, the variations in tone and character of white finishes can be a problem— buying everything from the same source can help.

Above: *Despite the uncompromising whiteness of this interior, it looks peaceful and cool rather than cold.*

Highlight

Even those who prefer a little color in their lives will often opt for white in a bathroom or kitchen, where it is a natural choice for fittings, appliances, and tiling. In functional rooms like these, in which the term "clinical" is a compliment and not a criticism, white also looks businesslike and efficient. Shiny surfaces are practical and normally easy to clean, though it is worth bearing in mind that they do show dirt and fingermarks and will therefore need regular maintenance.

The high-gloss, high-tech, high-spec look isn't confined to modern and minimal and doesn't preclude those with a taste for the old and traditional. Paintwork and floors covered with thick white gloss paint look wonderful in any situation, from a house with beautiful architectural details to a small cottage in need of brightening up. It's also a great way to add much-needed gloss to a featureless modern property.

SHINING EXAMPLES

Glazes
Use glazed tiles in bathrooms and kitchens. You can't go wrong with traditional square tiles, but look out for rectangular shapes, too. For a grown-up look, finish the edges with a molded edging tile. Shiny tiles on a floor can be a safety hazard, but nonslip surfaces are available to enable you to complete the all-white look.

Glass and mirrors
Perfect shiny companions to white, mirrors reflect the glory of the white surroundings, and mirror tiles and white are a dazzling combination. Let white shine through glass, whether it's a glass shower cubicle or a glass-topped table.

Shiny metal
Sparkling chrome, stainless steel, and aluminum keep white looking sharp. Complement the white with shiny fixtures, fittings, light fittings, and appliances and take your pick from the wide range of lampshades, picture frames, storage containers, vases, bowls, bins, and tableware. Though it is particularly effective in bathrooms and kitchens, shiny metal adds its sparkle to other areas and products, too, including furniture, not only as table and chair frames but also whole pieces such as chairs, stools, tables, and cabinets.

Super-shiny finishes
Units with a high-gloss-painted or spray-painted finish give an aura of high quality to kitchen units and furniture, and several coats of high-gloss paint is a great way to rejuvenate floors and old furniture.

Acrylics
Smooth and classy, especially when used for curvy molded furniture, acrylics can also be crisp and hard-edged for smart accessories and storage. Acrylic sheeting can be used for backsplashes or screens.

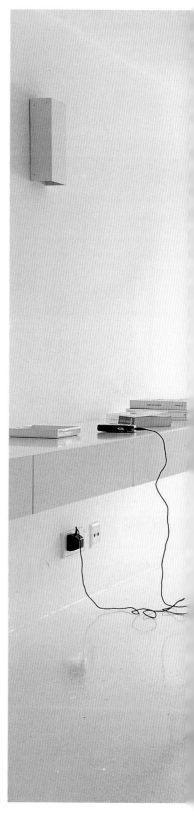

Right: *This wonderful glossy white floor turns an apparently ordinary space into something quite stunning and its impact is increased by the deliberately minimal style of the fittings and furnishings.*

Lowlight

While it is true that white can look cold and unfriendly, it is possible to create a mainly white interior that is warm and even cozy—think creamy whites, the color of white chocolate, vanilla ice cream, and undyed wool.

White can be warmed in several different ways. When it comes to paint, avoid brilliant white, which, with its touch of blue, is cool and unforgiving, and choose instead white with a hint of beige or warm yellow. (However, if your room has a sunny aspect, test these colors first as the cream could become too rich.) Some of the yellow tints added to white paint can be at the colder, greenish end and will create a chill rather than warmth. There are plenty of warmer whites in the "historic" ranges that use warm yellow ocher as a pigment and a base that is gray rather than dead white.

Warm whites tend to have a softening effect and can make a modern interior or a characterless space feel less intimidating. They are also more suitable in older properties where dead white feels too harsh. Sometimes a bright white, brightly lit interior is the right choice for a kitchen, bathroom, or work space, but for more relaxing activities such as dining, a long bath, or some quiet reading, you can calm things down by using softer lighting.

HOW TO WARM UP WHITE

- Choose warm white and cream shades for paints and textiles.

- Filter the natural light through warm-toned window coverings such as creamy gauze, unbleached linen, or wooden slatted shades.

- Use warm lighting—table lamps with warm-colored paper, parchment or tinted glass shades.

- Accessorize with warm ochers, oranges, beiges, and reds as well as plums and warm purples.

- Add firelight and candlelight for a comfortable warming glow.

- Team white with warm wooden floors, fixtures and fittings, furniture, and accessories.

- Choose a "soft" decorative style—old furniture, antiques, and faded textiles have a mellowing effect.

- Literally add warmth in the form of woollen fabrics for upholstery throws, cushions, and window coverings and carpet for floors.

Crisp and Even

When it comes to accessories, there is some truth in the saying that you can't go wrong with white, especially when buying inexpensive items, and this is certainly true of china, bed linen, fabrics, drapes, and window shades. Adding white accessories to a white interior will help to maintain the aura of order and cleanliness. Color is not banned but introducing color into a white room could spoil the atmosphere.

KEEP IT WHITE

Kitchen

Use white dishtowels, and make café drapes by clipping dishtowels onto a wire. Cover nonwhite table tops with white PVC-backed cloth or a cotton or linen tablecloth. Use white napkins and crockery and eschew stainless steel appliances and light fittings in favor of white. Not everything on open shelves has to be white—that would look too self-conscious—just make sure the shelves are white. If you do want to hide unattractive stuff, put it into white containers such as food storage jars, baskets, and bowls.

Bedrooms

Opt for white bed linen, bedcovers, and cushions. Dress windows with white floaty voile, plain white linen or cotton drapes, white fabric window shades or smart, white metal slatted shades. Keep to white light fittings and lampshades in fabric or paper. White baskets make attractive and unobtrusive storage.

Bathrooms

Use white fluffy towels and make sure washcloths, shower curtains, and bath mats are white, too. For windows, choose white shades or make a simple drape using a white cotton towel hung over a pole or clipped to a wire. Alternatively, you can't go wrong with white slatted shades. Extend the white theme to fittings such as towel rails and light fittings including frosted glass. Finally, keep clutter under control in white painted wood, plastic, or metal cupboards, shelves, drawers, and plastic or basketware containers.

Living areas

Unlike white shoes, which are guaranteed to make your feet look huge, white upholstery looks less heavy as well as very chic. If, however, white is too impractical for you, opt for white throws and cushion covers in washable fabrics. As in a bedroom, you can maintain privacy and dress windows with white voile or, for a more formal look, choose lined drapes or Roman blinds made up in a heavier fabric. White roller shades always look crisp and neat, as do white lampshades. White carpet is great for clean, well-behaved people but white (washable) rugs are a more practical alternative. If you want to be purist in your decoration, stick to white accessories—there are plenty of gorgeous white vases and objects to choose from.

Above: *This austere space with its hard surfaces is softened by the extensive use of white fabric for the drapes and throw. The white paper lampshades are the perfect choice as they create a soft form of lighting.*

Opposite: *The use of any soft furnishings other than a crisp, freshly ironed bedspread would have disturbed the tranquility of this beautifully simple bedroom.*

3

jeans and white t-shirt

blue and white china

black and white

Mondrian

WHITE PLUS

snowdrops

peppers and rice

strawberries and ice cream

bread and jelly

Even if an all-white interior isn't for you, white still provides a good foundation for an uncomplicated color scheme. White keeps things looking crisp and clean and can act as a unifying presence to tie in different colors throughout a whole house. Using it as the basis of an interior scheme also helps keep additional color under control and prevents it from dominating. You don't have to stick to just one extra color but it's best not to use more than two otherwise the look can get out of control. This is not as restrictive as it sounds because there are hundreds of shades within each color to keep things interesting and lively.

One of the simplest ways to liven up an interior is to paint one wall of a white room in another color. Picking out one area in paint or gorgeous wallpaper immediately changes the atmosphere and you can take things further by using shades and tones of the same color in furniture, furnishings, and accessories. When it comes to bright colors, pepper red, sunshine yellow, canteloupe, and pistachio green look great in a kitchen, while crimson and violet will add sophistication to a living room. You can experiment with the more difficult aquamarines and turquoises in a dining room, hallway, or bathroom. Choose a bright color that suits your personality and that will have a positive affect on your mood, not just one that is fashionable—fabulous shades look great in the right place but that may be on a sweater rather than in your kitchen or living room.

If you prefer subtle to stark contrast, pick a softer color for a gentler, less dramatic intervention. There are many wonderfully muted colors to choose from that might be too dark or somber as an all-over look but that will add a touch of sophistication to what might otherwise be a rather mediocre scheme.

When choosing the "plus" element, don't forget to take into consideration the color of other features in the interior such as floor finishes, furnishings, and fixtures and fittings. If these are dark or a definite color then any added color should be a variation on this theme—remember that too many plusses can add up to a minus! Whatever additional color you choose, the impact will be more effective if you follow a few guidelines.

Opposite: *Beyond this room, the inky blue dining area has the air of a secret grotto while the dark tones of the stairs and wood paneling make them appear sculptural against the white walls.*

White Plus Red

White plus red is a potent combination and guaranteed to make quite an impact in any room. Red is cheerful and invigorating, responds well to light, and works well by day and night—though it will look darker at night. What red you choose will depend on the context and your personal preference but because it is such a powerful color, red needs to be used with care.

Bright, clear reds work well in a kitchen—think red bell peppers and tomatoes—but a deeper tone may be more restful in a living room. Red is not an obvious choice for a bedroom, where a calm atmosphere is conducive to sleep, but bedrooms are not always just for sleeping and a lively color on one wall or a bedcover will relieve the coldness of an all-white environment. If you do choose to use red as a bedroom plus, you would be wise to put the red on the wall behind the bed so that it won't distract when you are trying to sleep.

INTRODUCING RED

Red's cheerfulness somehow stops it being oppressive but it is the color with the longest wavelength and will appear to come "forward" so bear this in mind when planning how and where to use it. You can lessen this forward effect by avoiding painting the wall that faces you on entering the room, or is facing you when you use the room—a sideways look may be less distracting and more restful. Red can make a small room feel smaller, while using a bright color on the longest wall in a long, narrow room will make the space feel even narrower. Painting the shorter wall in a bright color will help put things into proportion.

Painting one wall is a popular and easy way to introduce a bright color but paint isn't the only way to add red: a red tiled backsplash, floor, kitchen units, or furniture are other options. If you opt for red units, they really need to be the star attraction and so will work better in a disciplined, uncluttered space where they can stand out against a pristine white background.

Blocks of color work better than smaller bits and pieces, which is why red kitchen units work well, as would a large sofa, bed, or rug. Smaller items of furniture create a more fragmented color statement and therefore would benefit from being set off against a wall or floor of the same color.

Red can look harsh, so add other colors to soften the impact. Golden yellows, oranges, purples, and pinks work best and wood has a similar effect.

Above: *A glowing red box set into this kitchen turns dishwashing and cooking into a pleasure rather than a chore. The shelves provide a perfect backdrop for white china.*

Opposite: *In this living room, a curved wall has been painted in a brilliant glossy red. The dark floor and sofas create an air of sophistication, while the cushions provide extra color and luxury.*

Above: *This colorful collection of accessories adheres to a strict color code and therefore makes a bold statement against the all-white background.*

Below right: *The textured weave of the striped rug complements the stripped wood floor and provides a cheerful diversion from what could otherwise be an austere bedroom.*

Opposite: *Drapes and a textured wall help to soften this interior, while the red bedcover adds weight and color.*

ACCESSORIZE WITH RED

We all know how clever accessorizing can brighten up a dull outfit or give a twist to something plain, and something as simple as a colored scarf tied in a certain way can transform last year's fashion into this year's latest look. The style of an accessory can also dictate the look—a smart pair of shoes in this season's color adds chic, while a length of brightly colored ethnic cotton tied around the head or the waist looks more casual and more fun. The same applies to interiors, and using accessories as the plus in a white interior can work the same magic.

As with fashion, it is wise not to get carried away and overdo things—a pair of bright red shoes with an all-white outfit can look sensational but adding a red scarf, a hat, and bag would look silly and would diminish the effect. Similarly, a single red rug can work wonders, as could a single stunning red vase, and this is because one block of color or a playful splash makes more of an impact. In a kitchen, a row of red mugs looks great, but start dotting around red cutting boards, dishtowels, utensils, trays, storage jars, and any more of the tempting array of colored accessories that we find so hard to resist and it starts to look messy.

Think carefully about how and where you position these accent accessories. If you group a collection of red objects together on a set of shelves, for example, it will look clever and considered rather than messy. And while a single red rug might look lost on the floor, it could have a big impact hung on the wall.

Rugs and carpets

Lots of modern designs are bright and bold and they are sometimes surprisingly inexpensive. Look in flea markets and antique markets for old rugs, kilims, and nonfitted carpets and keep an eye out for rag rugs. Oriental carpets go with anything and always look good, while kilims and dhurries are often cheap and cheerful and available in good colors.

Ceramics and glass

These are a good way to add splashes of color, but don't go over the top—remember it's a home not a show house. If you favor a large collection, include a variety of shades and tones of one or two colors.

Cushions

Cushions provide an easy way to use bright colors and patterns, but again, don't overdo it. Keep the colors under control: it's much better to have three with the same or similar coloring plus one different than four distinct colors. And resist the temptation to cover everything in cushions, which not only looks messy but can actually make chairs and sofas quite uncomfortable.

Throws and bedcovers

The perfect opportunity for making a color statement and one that allows you to experiment with colors you would be too afraid to commit to a wall. Throws and bedcovers provide a flexible way of adding color that allows you to ring the changes seasonally.

White Plus Green

Green is a color that we love to have around us in the form of trees and plants and it is generally accepted that green can have a beneficial effect on our well-being. Green is also associated with freshness—think of leafy glades or leafy vegetables—and nowadays the word green is also used to describe awareness of, and respect for, the environment.

You only have to look at a garden or landscape to realize how many shades of green there are. Green is created by mixing blue and yellow together, so it is obvious that those shades that contain more blue will be cooler and those with more yellow in them will appear warmer. Many shades of green also contain small amounts of red, which warms them up and prevents them from being too harsh.

Which green you choose will depend on your personal preference and where in your home you plan to use it, but green can be a difficult color to get right because it changes its nature in different situations. Bright and dark greens can be particularly tricky as they can be cold, and the deeper shades used in any quantity can overwhelm. Green can make a room with small windows look gloomy, and at night, a bright green can change into something quite dark. It is also worth noting that green will cast its hue on everything around it—including people.

However, when used alongside plenty of white, green can look clean and crisp. For a stark contrast, the brighter greens are best used in places such as kitchens, while the darker shades can work well in a living room. As with any color, particularly strong ones, it's a good idea to buy sample pots of different shades and try them out before making your final choice.

GREEN GAUGE

Grass
From the vibrancy of new spring grass to the gentler hues of summer meadows, this shade is great with white in kitchens, but it needs a sunny aspect—in a north-facing room it can feel very cold and looks darker. If you think of grass with flowers and blue sky you realize that any color will go with it.

Lime
Lime is a bright and cheerful color with dramatic tendencies and the right shade can work well in any room. However, it can lose its intensity in the absence of light or if it is too yellowy or has too much white or gray in it.

Forest
Dark green is a grown-up color and can look very sophisticated in an elegant living room or dining room. It works best in spaces with high ceilings and plenty of light.

Olive
A more muted, yellowy green, which is warm and friendly. Olives can look dull without sunshine, though, and so will benefit from the addition of one or two other lively or clean colors. This is a good color for living areas, especially as part of a retro scheme.

Blue-green
Blue-greens—from deep sea to emerald—can be cool and refreshing when in the presence of plenty of light and white and are therefore perfect for bathrooms. But they can also look wonderfully rich in a more traditional setting with antiques, luxurious fabrics, printed fabric, and wallpaper.

WHITE PLUS GREEN PLUS...

White and green on their own can sometimes look a little austere, but introducing a third color will liven things up. There are many options:

- **Orange**—a tangy addition

- **Mustard**—from the hot yellow English to the milder French

- **Pale blue**—cleans and refreshes

- **Salmon**—the perfect accompaniment to lime and lettuce

- **Shocking pink**—livens things up

- **Rose pink**—a natural, and romantic, combination

Above: A bedhead provides a good opportunity to introduce a small but dramatic splash of bold color into a room, especially when used with crisp white bed linen.

MAKE IT WORK FOR YOU

White Plus Green Plus Red

Bold use of color can change a perfectly nice white kitchen into something quite special. Bright color works best if you apply it in one or possibly two designated areas so avoid the temptation to dot extra dabs of that color elsewhere.

Green can be overwhelming when used in large expanses, but in a mainly white kitchen with white units it looks appropriately fresh and crisp. In this kitchen, the green panel above the sink appears lighter than the color on the other wall owing to the light thrown on it from the side and without this light source alongside the sink, it is possible that the green above would have looked oppressive.

Green and white on their own can look a little cold and stark, which is why bringing in another strong color, preferably something warm, is a good idea. Red and green together often have a dizzying effect on the eye that is anything but restful, but in this kitchen, where red has been added in the form of curvy acrylic furniture, the red is comfortably warm, and the reflective surface further softens the color. If the floor had been white, the red and green would almost certainly have vied with one another for attention but here the dark floor calms things down.

Opposite: This kitchen looks pristine and functional, but with the addition of cheerful red furniture, it takes on a warm and friendly ambience.

COLOR PALETTE

Lime green	Bright green	Red	Brown black	White
These yellowy greens add zest to any interior and, being lighter, work better than a grass green in a dark space. This paler green also works well with red.	*Clear, pure green looks fresh and clean but needs white to keep it bright. Like most bright colors, this green looks better in large blocks than in smaller areas.*	*This pure bright red, which looks as if it has come straight out of a paint tube, is warm and friendly as it leans toward yellow rather than blue.*	*Black is not only black: it contains other colors, which change its character accordingly. Brown-black is warmer and has a softening effect on the stark green, red, and white.*	*Pure, bright, cool white is the right white to keep things looking clean and fresh. It is the shade most commonly used for smooth man-made materials found in kitchen fittings and appliances.*

ADDED INGREDIENTS

Stainless steel
Shiny and bright, it reflects the surrounding colors and keeps everything looking light. It sharpens up the white units and looks functional and efficient. Using it for the shelves and as a backsplash keeps the number of different elements to a minimum.

Pictures
Placing a mainly white picture on the green wall adds light relief and stops the green from looking too heavy.

Furniture
This uncompromisingly modern furniture in wipe-down acrylic combines fun with functional, and opting for stools rather than chairs keeps things looking neat.

Floor
The shiny surface of this floor echoes the rest of the furniture and fittings, but a wooden or tiled floor would work just as well. Choose a dark color to help ground a brightly colored room.

White Plus Blue

Anyone who has traveled to hot, sunny countries such as Greece cannot fail to be enchanted by the simple vernacular architecture, much of which is painted pristine white with details picked out in deep blue.

In Mediterranean countries, blue helps to bring the temperature down, but in more northerly climes, it can be a cold, hard color. Nevertheless, blue is a natural companion for white, whether it is adding a dash of authority to a uniform or gentle prettiness to a china teacup.

Pure blues include Prussian blue, ultramarine, lapis lazuli, and the softer indigo, but in the color wheel blue goes from the deepest blue green to darkest purple and it is a main component in a wide palette ranging from turquoise to lavender. Dark or bright pure blues can be chilly, but the grayer blues, such as those found in traditional paints, can be wonderfully warm, and because blue "recedes," you can get away with slightly darker shades in a small room.

BLUE MOODS

Blue and white is a classic color combination that can be found in many guises, including favorite outfits and everyday objects, and can form the basis of a variety of different decorating styles.

Denim and white
Think how timeless the jeans and white shirt look is: it never goes out of fashion, looks good in almost any situation, and always feels comfortable. Denim is strong and hardwearing and great for upholstery, throws, cushion covers, and drapes. And if you are handy with a needle, why not make throws and bedcovers (line them with fleece for extra warmth) and big bags for linen or for storing clothes, toys, sewing, spare bed linen, and anything else that needs a place to hide?

Blue and white stripes
From the bold blue of butchers' stripes to the neatness of ticking, blue and white stripes are ideal for upholstery, cushions, drapes, and shades. Roman blinds made from crisp white ticking with a narrow blue stripe add just enough blue to sharpen up a white room. It's easy to find blue and white stripes in a variety of fabrics—and don't forget checks and spots either.

Blue and white china
For a feminine touch, take inspiration from Delft, willow pattern, country scenes, pretty florals on porcelain, and functional chunky deep-blue glazed pots and pitchers. The deep intense blue used for decoration on ceramics is provided by the use of cobalt, which contrasts beautifully with the white background. For a smart, sophisticated look in a bathroom, top off white tiles with a narrow border of dark blue edging tiles.

Lavender and lace
Pretty, romantic, nostalgic; call it what you will, a white room dressed in pretty lavender blue and white florals, some toiles de Jouy, and a little lace is irresistably charming and a look that is not difficult to achieve.

Abstract expression
If you are into art and modernism, why not paint a wall in Yves Klein blue? This dense but brilliant color will make a huge impact, which is the whole point.

White and Dark

A very dark color added to a mostly white interior is bound to have great impact, especially when used over an extensive area such as a wall, ceiling, or floor. This dramatic effect is often used by architects and designers in large, modern interiors to manipulate the space. A dark ceiling will appear lower and a dark floor makes a space feel smaller, both useful devices for making big spaces feel more human in scale. Deep-colored walls have a similar effect. Think carefully before using dark colors in a small room, where the result can be claustrophobic.

As with most bold uses of color, discipline is required, a small palette is essential and a pared-down, uncluttered environment the recommended style. There are many ways to introduce a dark element into an interior scheme, including paint, dark wood, and fabrics. Good paint colors include dark browns, battleship grays, and midnight blues, plus all the different versions of black from steely blue-black to dramatic purple-black.

A white and dark theme is perfect for modern, pared-down interiors but it can also look elegant and sophisticated in older houses and with old and antique furnishings. As with bright colors, it is important to use a dark color in blocks; small amounts will not work effectively. A dark wall is a perfect backdrop for beautiful furniture of any style while a white room looks wonderful with slabs of dark, sleek modern furniture and upholstery, especially if they're placed on a white floor. Dark drapes and shades can look bleak against a blank white wall and therefore should not be used as the only dark element in a room. They will work much better if the floor and some of the furnishings are also dark.

When using dark colors, it is important to get the right balance of light and dark in the interior as a whole. Dark is heavy, so keeping dark colors to the lower part of a room, leaving plenty of white above, will keep things looking light. A dark floor on its own in a white space can look a bit lost, so give it a purpose by including it as part of a scheme that features other dark elements such as furniture and fittings.

Dark colors can be difficult to spend a lot of time with, which is why a bathroom is a good place to try them out; the plain shapes of fittings will look good against a dark background. Dark base units in a kitchen can look great, but dark wall cupboards could be too overpowering, so either confine cupboards to one wall or, if you have high ceilings, leave a space between the top of the cupboards and the ceiling. A white floor could also help to maintain balance.

When it comes to finishes, matte latex and wool, linen, and thick cotton upholstery fabrics look chic but so, too, do glossy surfaces, and these will also reflect the light.

Right: *This minimal kitchen has obviously been designed to be functional, yet it is also beautiful. Nothing is allowed to detract from the impact of a slab of dark color set in a white environment. The concealed lighting prevents it looking too austere.*

Above: *The walls of this bathroom have been painted a similar dark color to the countertop. Keeping to white accessories makes everything look crisp and fresh.*

Opposite: *The warmth of the dark, well-worn wooden floor prevents this resolutely minimal interior from looking too cold and clinical. It also provides a contrasting texture to the smooth finishes of the furniture and paintwork.*

DARK MATERIALS

Our obsession with the light and airy means that we often neglect or dismiss dark materials as too heavy, which is a shame—those such as dark woods and stone have wonderful qualities as well as beautifully subtle coloring.

Wood
Dark wood has an essentially warm feel, which is why it works so well in a modern, pared-down interior. There is a huge variety of solid woods and veneers available, with colors ranging from almost black to deep nut browns. The natural graining in wood provides texture as well as surface interest and prevents even very dark wood from looking too heavy. In both old houses and more prosaic homes, dark wood floors and furniture provide character as well as warmth, and wood has a mellowing effect on stark white paint. A dark wood floor can make a room look small but dark wood furniture, whether modern or antique, stands out

beautifully against a white background. Many contemporary interiors feature dark wood paneling, which looks smart and sophisticated when used in moderation with plenty of white.

Stone and composites
Stone is increasingly being used in interiors and in more adventurous ways, and dark stone has a distinctive, solid, and practical presence that adds weight as well as contrast to a mainly white interior. Granites, slates, and marbles can be found in a subtle range of colors, including black, gray, dark greens, and deep reds, and in a choice of polished, matte, and textured finishes. There are also several composites and ceramics that look like stone, some of which are cheaper and more practical than the real thing. As well as fireplaces, countertops, backsplashes, and surrounds, it is also possible to get sinks and bathtubs that are made out of stone or stonelike materials. Stone is available in large sheets, cut or molded forms, and tiles.

Paint
Unless we are painting a front door or the yard gate, we seldom explore the darker end of the paint charts, fearing that such colors would be just too overpowering in a domestic interior. While it is true that very deep colors should be used with caution as they absorb light, bring walls in, and ceilings down, they also lend dramatic relief to a bland white space. Dark browns, grays, and even black can look chic and sophisticated, but these colors do work better in a simple, sparsely furnished interior. Go for cool browns that have a touch of gray, and grays that are slightly warm. If you are brave enough to use black, you will find a selection, from warm browny black to steely blue-black and those with a greeny tinge.

Paint comes in several different finishes. A gloss-painted dark wall will

make a very bold statement and the fact that it reflects light can make it appear less dark, but a matte finish gives a more subtle effect.

Wallpaper

A bold wallpaper can make quite an impact on a room and whereas a painted wall is a solid block of color, a patterned paper is less heavy. While dark wallpaper may be too much for a whole room, it can look fabulous as the dark interest on one wall of a white room. Look for damask patterns on dark backgrounds and retro sixties patterns with lots of dark browns and greens. The deep blues and greens in dark William Morris prints still look great even in a modern setting, and now that wallpaper is hot once more, there are plenty of fantastic new options to choose from.

Textiles

Dark-colored upholstery, carpets, rugs, drapes, and shades add substance to a white room, but smaller items look better if they are grouped together to form a solid block of color rather than used in isolation. Dark carpets can look great when newly vacuumed, but they do show the bits; dark woollen rugs, either plain or patterned, are generally more practical. For upholstery and window coverings, look for smooth plain wools and tweeds in browns and grays, or for a more glamorous or traditional look, choose velvets and damasks. Plains are good, but dark patterns provide extra interest and relief to lighten the atmosphere.

Metal

Instead of shiny, go for dark, painted metal and enameled finishes such as those used on range cookers and metal funiture. Wrought iron is naturally dark and rustic, and ethnic metal furniture and accessories have a dark patina that stands out beautifully in a white interior.

Left: *The dark wooden floor and imposing leather sofa add extra luxury to this classy bathroom, as do the carefully positioned shelves and their contents.*

Below left: *The stark simplicity of the white sofa stands out beautifully against the dark wall. The patterned rug and striped lampshade bring in other dark touches.*

Opposite: *In another situation, dark structural beams together with dark upholstery could look very heavy. Here, however, the huge windows and white floor prevent these dark areas from looking oppressive. Instead, they complement and emphasize the architecture.*

Subtle Contrast

Sometimes painting everything white is the easiest and most successful way in which to bring a sense of order to a home. White can disguise inadequacies, lighten dark spaces, enlarge small ones, and discipline awkward ones, and it is also good for unifying an otherwise disorderly interior or collection of items. But if you want a little relief from white and prefer subtle rather than stark contrast, there are various ways to do it.

Maintaining an aura of calm is a priority and therefore any deviation from white needs to blend in rather than stand out. Remember that color doesn't necessarily have to be in the form of paint or fabric: materials such as wood and stone also have color and can play their role. Adding a few gentle-toned fabrics, colored walls, or a wooden floor to a white interior will make it feel less austere without losing the sense of space.

SUBTLE DISTINCTIONS

Wood
A wooden floor is the perfect way to soften an all-white space, but for subtlety, choose the lighter colors and finishes. If you are stripping the floors, finish them with a clear varnish or oil, and think about treating doors, window frames, and any wooden paneliing in the same way. Make light-colored wood the material of choice for floors, shelving, furniture, kitchen units, and fixtures, fittings, and accessories.

Wallpaper
Pale-colored prints on white backgrounds are ideal for prettying up a bedroom and you could use bolder designs in subtle colors on a single wall in a living area or hallway.

Painted surfaces
Use subtle colors such as darker "old" whites, creams, pale grays, beiges, blues, and greens on walls, woodwork, floors, and furniture. In a white kitchen, pale green or blue units look fresh and clean. In a bathroom, pale green tiles look relaxing and smart.

Softeners
Fabrics, cushions, throws, drapes, shades, wallhangings, carpets, and rugs make things feel as well as look softer. Natural and unbleached cottons and linens and undyed wools are great for warming up white, and the different shades and tones of natural fabrics and fibers work together to create harmony. If bare floors are too hard or noisy, natural-fiber floor coverings such as sea grass and sisal are a good alternative. When it comes to colored textiles, natural fibers take dye in such a way as to give a deeper, more subtle color.

Below left: *Using accessories in different textures and materials is a good way to introduce subtle contrast within a very small color range.*

Opposite: *Apart from the bathtub, all the elements in this bathroom share a similar tonal quality. The mirror, though dramatic, provides subtle contrast in the form of reflected color.*

Splash it About

Adding color to white doesn't necessarily require restraint, but you will need to exercise a little self-discipline with larger splashes of color to prevent things getting out of hand. Confining the color to a single area, level, or plane will ensure maximum impact. Even a joyful riot of colorful furniture can be tamed if the height of the various pieces—particularly seat-back height—is roughly the same, and if other colorful distractions are not allowed to stray above that line. A dark or similarly colored floor will also help to hold the color down in its defined area and give a more cohesive result.

SPLASH, DON'T SPLATTER

Avoid the temptation to dot small bits of color around, which will result in an unfocused look. The important thing is to keep control and to use color in large areas such as upholstery, pieces of furniture, rugs, and perhaps some pictures. It also helps if you obey the rule of limiting the palette to one or two strong colors plus shades and tones of those colors. When choosing your colors, don't forget to take into consideration other color elements in the room such as furniture, fittings, and the floor.

Opposite: *This unusual artwork was clearly the source of the deceptively disciplined color scheme here—the colors of all the various accessories are to be found in the painting.*

FAMILY TIES

Confining yourself to even just one strong color still allows plenty of scope for colorful compositions. Consider some of the other colors tied to these primaries, for example:

- **Bright yellow**—egg-yolk yellow, mustard, pale yellow, lemon, lime, orange, burnt orange.

- **Bright red**—deep red, maroon, pinks, red-purple, mauves.

- **Bright blue**—dark blues, pale blues, turquoise, blue-greens, blue-grays, blue-purple.

- **Bright green**—forest green, blue-greens, pale greens, lime, gray-greens.

CHEAP AND CHEERFUL

Sometimes the simplest things give the most pleasure for least amount of effort. It's easy and fun to cheer up a plain white interior with a pot of paint and a few colorful accessories. Choose a small but cheerful palette of colors that includes one paint color and a collection of fabrics containing either that color or contrasting ones in similar tones.

Painting furniture is an easy way to add color: paint a single chair, a dresser, a mirror, or a large picture frame or collection of small ones. Flea market finds are perfect for this sort of makeover but cheap new equivalents can be given a fresh personality with a coat of paint. Complete the splash of color with a collection of cushions and perhaps one or two accessories such as a basket or small table. This approach is good in bathrooms, kitchens, and bedrooms where a more relaxed look is more appropriate. In a living room, you can make bigger splashes with a bigger mirror, pictures, a sofa, and cushions, and perhaps a rug.

MODERN MANNERS

When the Modernists designed their simple, elegant furniture (much of which is still available today), they also developed a fashion for painting rooms white. But in fact the Modernists did have color in their homes and they placed their designs among beautiful—and colorful—objects and artworks. Today, architects, designers, and lovers of all things modern often favor the stark white, minimalist box in which to display their treasures. However, your surroundings say much about you, and if you're not careful, an all-white interior could give the impression that you are either unimaginative or frightened to show your real personality.

Left: *This bathroom has been cheered up with summertime colors, including limy and grass greens, warm sunny yellow, and some hot pink stripes and checks.*

Below left: *The colored chairs and tabletop are allowed to be the center of attraction in this understated environment—even the carefully arranged objects are uniformly muted.*

Above: *White is the perfect choice as a backdrop to this collection of mostly modern furniture, pictures, and objects, but the wooden floor and shelving help create an overall impression of warmth and comfort.*

Modern furniture can look very severe and unwelcoming in a white space so it will benefit from the company of a few of your favorite things. The perfect way to display a collection of pictures or objects is on shelves and it works best if you restrict shelving to one wall or section of wall and treat that area as an art installation. Paintings look great if they are propped up on a narrow shelf rather than hung on the wall. A collection of pictures gathered together in one area looks more interesting than dotting them around the room and allows you to change the displays frequently without making holes in the wall. It also enables you to keep the other walls free of pictures in modern, minimalist fashion. You don't have to follow a color theme—if pictures are good they will work well together no matter what their subject or coloring—though if you want to play the coordination game, that's fine. You can also use the colors in the pictures or objects as a palette for cushions and throws, but remember to keep it simple.

MAKE IT WORK FOR YOU

Splash it About

Confined to one end of an otherwise all-white space, what appears as an extremely exuberant burst of color is in fact quite disciplined. The vibrant pink takes center stage: it can't be ignored and so the other colors have been carefully chosen so as not to compete for attention. A relatively small area of hot pink is on show—any more and it would be overpowering—and if it wasn't for the unconventional patchwork quilt with its dark reds, purply browns, and acid greens, it would take over completely. Although the pink is undoubtedly bright and the whole picture makes a real splash, the colors of the other cushions are in fact quite restrained. The amethyst is a slightly pinky version of purple, similar in tone to the lighter pink, which means that they harmonize rather than shout.

The reason this scheme works so well and looks so dramatic is that it is confined to a relatively small area. Use of the brightest color is restricted and the patchwork cover made up of squares of several colors work better than one slab of color. The rest of the space is uncompromisingly white and the temptation to take the color theme elsewhere has been resisted. A colored lampshade, a pink rug, or bright drapes would have spoiled the effect completely. The picture is the only other source of color but positioned above the divan it is part of the whole scene rather than a distraction.

Opposite: Despite the stark whiteness of its surroundings, this colorful niche looks both cheerful and inviting—the perfect place for a quiet read or a cozy chat.

COLOR PALETTE

Vivid pink	**Pale pink**	**Amethyst**	**Pale lime**	**Chocolate brown**
A loud color that demands attention and certainly gets it in a white setting. It requires careful handling and is best used in controlled amounts.	*Adding white to vivid pink could be a bit sugary so choose a subtler version that calms it down with a touch of gray.*	*Hovering between purple, pink, and blue, this is the perfect color to tone down the excesses of bright pinks or purples.*	*Lime green offers a refreshing antidote to pink, but with vivid pink, a paler lime is best—it will complement it rather than trying to compete.*	*Used in small quantities, the rich tones of chocolate add warmth and weight, preventing pink from being too overpowering.*

Shock Tactics

The great fashion commentator Diana Vreeland famously called shocking pink the navy blue of India, and wearing it—or using it in your home—does require a certain amount of good fashion sense. Like navy blue, shocking pink is perfect with white, but unlike navy, which can form the basis of an outfit, bright pink is more of an accessory color to be used with flair and confidence. For interiors, shocking takes the girly out of pink: it is still feminine but more strong woman than dizzy blonde and more chic than chick, though hippie can be hip.

Pink can be a bit much on walls, so use it as you would with clothes—a jacket, shirt, or scarf, but not the whole outfit. One of the best places to use shocking pink is on upholstery. Thick cottons, linens, and wool give depth to the color, and used on a sofa, armchair, or a bedhead it makes a good solid splash against a white background.

As shocking pink is such a dominant color, the no-clutter rule is best obeyed, but if you do want to add other colors, go for refreshment in the form of lime greens, acid yellows, and even a dash of turquoise, or take a more subtle approach with amethyst, purple, and paler pinks. Pink in a white interior, especially if the floor is white too, certainly can't be ignored, but it can look more grown-up and sophisticated on a dark floor.

IN THE PINK

Pink chic

Maintain your composure in elegant surroundings with just the right amount of pink to show your wilder side. Keep it smart with smooth fabrics, clean lines, and disciplined simplicity. Make pink and white sophisticated by teaming it with dark wood, stainless steel, and chrome and a few well-chosen white accessories.

Pink hippie

Connect with your inner hippie and kick against the anticlutter brigade with a comfy casual look. Pick out the shocking pink with floaty voile at the window or even around a bed, kilims and dhurries, ethnic objects, baskets, and jolly plastics. Keep the pink dominance in check with flashes of turquoise, lime greens, and amethyst.

Pink glamour

Glam it up and embellish your white interior with luxury fabrics—think pink velvets, silks, satins, and damask—a few ornate objects and a touch of gold. If you are feeling adventurous, you can add a wall of pink patterned wallpaper or, if you really want to shock, over-long, heavy, silk damask drapes hung from a gilded pole. Add one or two elaborate pieces of furniture and accessorize with gilded picture frames and mirrors, pretty lamps, and perhaps a chandelier.

Opposite: *The dark floor and modern furniture has a sobering effect on the pink sofa, making it appear smart and sophisticated rather than frivolous.*

Above: *The use of pink for the sofa, table, and delightfully quirky sculpture in an otherwise all-white room adds a touch of femininity and glamour.*

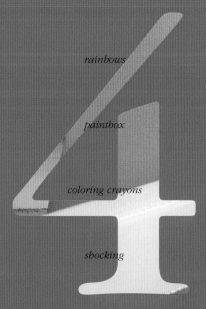

primary colors

rainbows

paintbox

coloring crayons

shocking

electric

GLORIOUS
TECHNICOLOR

startling

luminous

riot of color

Matisse

Monet

Kandinsky

If you love bright colors and like to surround yourself with them, don't be afraid to use them in your home. A vividly colored interior is not exactly relaxing, but it doesn't have to exhausting either, and there are things you can do to prevent your color wheel from spinning out of control.

If you are not sure how you want to color your particular world, take your inspiration from art. Look at the glorious colors in the paintings of Kandinsky, for example, or note Van Gogh's famous yellow chair and bed and the colorful, sunny California as painted by David Hockney. A postcard of a painting by a favorite artist provides a ready-made palette for a color scheme and is likely to be far more subtle and sophisticated than anything you could come up with on your own. You may also be surprised to find that the number of colors used is more restricted than you imagined and that many of the colors are more muted than they appear.

Colors react with one another in unexpected ways and play tricks on our eyes and brains. Placing colors next to one another often has surprising consequences with bright colors losing their intensity and apparently dull colors springing into life. A shiny color will look lighter than a matte finish while textures throw shadows and make colors appear darker. When using a colorful palette, the influence of light, position, and orientation of a room become even more pronounced and therefore it is very important to try out colors in their intended setting before committing to them.

The large numbers of paint colors, wallpapers, and textiles on offer is wide and wonderful, but if you are daunted by so much choice, try restricting your palette to products from a specific company, manufacturer, designer, or store as they are likely to all share similar characteristics of tone, style, and basic materials, which means that they will naturally work together.

Opposite: *Such a wonderfully bold use of color is the perfect way to make a feature of an area in the home that is often not given the attention it deserves.*

Primary School

In theory, any color can be made by mixing different amounts of red, blue, and yellow, which are known as primary colors. When it comes to interiors, don't get too hung up on the correct definition of "primary"—the term is often used to describe all the strong, bright colors, including green, violet, and orange, that are found in the rainbow. In their undiluted state, the characteristics of these colors will be reinforced. Red appears to come forward and blue recedes, and red, yellow, orange, and purple feel warm, while blue and green are cooler.

The strength of these colors means that they have a powerful effect on one another and they will vie with each other for attention. It is therefore advisable not to use too many in one area. Instead, include variations of the colors in the form of tints, tones, and shades, colors produced by adding white, gray, and black respectively.

Using strong colors takes nerve and some talent, so don't be afraid to enlist the help of people who know how to handle their color. For example, look at the paintings of Matisse, which are full of pure bright colors but also contain some wonderfully subtle ones that play an important role in the balance and composition. Include some of these in your palette to help you to create your own interior compositions.

Using primary colors with white (see chapter 3, White Plus) is perhaps the safest and easiest option, but for a more intense experience, be bold and use them as the main attraction and in larger quantities. Though bright colors are often associated with all things modern, color schemes of the past were often much more colorful and adventurous than those of more recent times: whole rooms in deep blues,

reds, and greens were a feature of stately homes as well as more modest houses. Today, many older properties are given a coat of white to make them look "modern" when in fact they would be more comfortable in colorful clothing. Similarly, bright colors add personality to new or more prosaic homes. Be brave: impress your friends (and yourself) with a sapphire blue or sunny yellow dining room, a bright red living room, a cobalt-blue bathroom, a purple bedroom, or a lime-green kitchen.

Studying the theory of color is one way of understanding how colors work with each other but it is a complex subject and is not necessarily the ideal way to discover what works best in a north-facing bedroom, for example. Choosing how to decorate your home is a combination of personal taste, natural instinct, and experience, and there is a lot to be said for doing your own thing rather than following the orders of strict interior advisers, especially as color—and our response to it—is a very personal thing. Nevertheless, a few facts and guidelines can be helpful.

Opposite: *A neutral background allows bright colors to shine. Here, the bright green and red stand out beautifully as they have nothing else to compete with.*

Below: *The use of red and black makes this a very dramatic interior redolent of old castles or palaces. The minimal furnishings help to maintain a feeling of space despite the dark colors.*

PAINTING CLASS

Faced with a paintbox of bright colors it is easy to get carried away and end up with a mess rather than a work of art. Following a few guidelines will help to ensure that your colorful ideas become successful color schemes.

- Don't use too many colors—the trick is to add interest in the form of tints, tones, and shades of one or two colors rather than a different primary.

- For a more restrained look, paint the walls in subtle or neutral shades and introduce bold color in the form of upholstery, rugs, drapes, shades, and accessories—but don't use too many different colors or it will look disjointed.

- Painting floors and furniture in bright primaries is a great way to add color as well as an economical way to make the most of what you've got.

- Avoid the temptation to populate brightly colored upholstery with a rainbow of colored cushions. It will look smarter with a collection of cushions in the same color or variations of that color, plus perhaps one bright contrast.

- If a bright color on every wall is too much, paint one wall bright and do the rest in a paler shade or tint or another subtle color.

- White makes colors look more intense and can create too much contrast. Brilliant colors will look more sophisticated when set against subtle colors such as beige and warm gray, and will respond well to the mellowing effects of wood floors and furniture.

- Instead of adding another color, use varieties of one color in the form of different textures and finishes. Add interest with gloss, eggshell, and matte paint, chunky and smooth textiles in rugs and upholstery, textured wall coverings, and colored furniture and accessories in a variety of materials, from smooth glass, metal, and plastics to rougher painted wood and baskets.

- Add pizzazz with brightly colored prints and patterns in the form of fabrics and wallpaper. Set them against a plain shade chosen from the colors contained in the pattern.

Above: *Blue and red can be difficult together, but here the brilliance of the kingfisher blue works beautifully against the earthy red.*

Opposite: *Shades of red are not an obvious choice for a bathroom but perhaps these wonderful old tiles were the inspiration. The pristine whiteness of the bathtub shines out against its dark surroundings.*

RED

- Primary attraction: yellow, orange, and purple

- Bright contrasts: bright pinks, brilliant blue

- Calming effects: pale pinks and mauves, brown, dark gray, deep purple

YELLOW

- Primary attraction: red, blue, purple, orange

- Bright contrasts: brilliant blue, violet

- Calming effects: pale blue, indigo, taupe, brown

BLUE

- Primary attraction: red, yellow, orange

- Bright contrasts: bright pink, lime green

- Calming effects: pink, mauve, brown, olive green, mustard

GREEN

- Primary attraction: yellow, red

- Bright contrasts: bright pink, light blue, bright mustard

- Calming effects: taupe, dark brown, deep purple

RED AND YELLOW

Reds and yellows are at the warm end of the color spectrum and therefore are a good way to bring cheer into your home. However, the strong presence of these colors can prove too overbearing if you are not careful.

Yellow is, on the whole, a happy color associated with sunshine, and it can indeed brighten up a dull or gloomy space. Intense yellows, such as egg yolk, veer toward orange and are therefore undoubtedly warm, but the more greeny yellows, such as lemon, can be surprisingly cool. Similarly, reds containing yellow are warm and soft whereas those containing a lot of blue are cooler and can look harsh.

Red is a popular and ubiquitous color. Most product ranges—whether of ceramics, fabrics, or furniture—will offer a choice of red. It also regularly crops up in patterns, where in combination with other colors, it adds depth, definition, and interest. Red works well with most colors but also looks good on its own. As paint or wallpaper, it can have a very grand appearance in a room with high ceilings and traditional or antique furniture, but it is also a good color for an intimate, cozy living room. However, bear in mind that, as red looks darker at night, a color that appears bright and cheerful in daylight could turn heavy and sinister in artificial light.

Yellow can look good almost anywhere, but an all-over, bright yellow experience can be too overpowering in a small room unless there are large windows and plenty of light. It is a softer option than red and is good for cheering up hallways and kitchens—and children love it in their bedrooms and playrooms. It is a mistake to think of yellow only in cheerful, sunny terms, however, as it can look wonderfully sophisticated and elegant in a high-ceilinged dining room or bedroom.

Opposite: This brilliant red and yellow bathroom with its mirror-tiled floor is quite outrageous and would certainly wake you up and cheer you up. Such a color scheme could be overwhelming, but as a bathroom is used for only short periods of time, it is a good place to be adventurous.

Vivid Scenes

Beautiful old houses deserve respect, but they don't have to remain trapped in the past. For some, not sticking to an historically correct color scheme may be seen as shocking and insensitive, but in fact the color schemes of the past were often much more colorful and exuberant than we, admiring of peeling paint and faded glories, realize. An over-the-top fantasy palette is not an easy thing to get right, but if you love that sort of thing, and think you could live with it, it's worth a try. You don't have to live in an architectural gem to get this style to work successfully, but you will have to moderate your colors and modify the look to suit a smaller space.

STRONG HINTS

Choose colors of similar intensity
Choosing colors with the same strength and characteristics is made easier with helpful paint color charts where the colors are divided into "families" and "moods," often with further categories based on how the colors are made up. Picking all the colors from one specific category ensures a consistent look. Some of the "historic" color charts are not divided in this way, but their colors already share quite a strong character, and as they normally contain more pigment, the strong colors are naturally intense.

Buy everything from one supplier
Paint colors vary depending on how they are made, and so by sticking to one manufacturer and production process, you can be sure that the products will be based on similar raw materials and therefore share the same characteristics and a similar look.

Use large areas of color
Don't paint woodwork in a different color unless you are fortunate enough to have generous, molded architraves, baseboards, and window frames. The narrow and rather mean moldings and characterless windows used in many modern houses won't stand up to the scrutiny of a contrasting color, so paint them the same color as the wall and use another color on the door or window reveal instead.

Keep furnishings to a minimum
The vivid scene is really is for those with minimalist tendencies as clutter will turn fantasy into horror. And don't attempt this if your furniture is not up to scratch. Far from drawing attention away from substandard stuff, a bold color scheme will show up all its deficiencies.

Don't forget the floor
Extending the color scheme to the floor will make the look more cohesive. If your existing floor is beautiful wood, stone, or tiles, think about using colorful rugs, but if the floor is not special, then you could paint it or put down a rubber or vinyl floor covering.

Above: *The brilliant pink throw gives the antique sofa a modern twist as does the unusual color scheme in this beautiful old house.*

Opposite: *Many would consider this wild and exuberant color scheme to be disrespectful to a house such as this, but in fact it creates a joyous ambience, which celebrates the wonderful architectural detailing.*

Purple Prose

A house with superb architectural features and detailing responds well to being decorated in an extraordinarily bold way. Dark saturated colors create an almost gothic atmosphere and painting a room in plum and black requires a certain amount of courage. You may not have such a distinctive home as the one shown opposite, but you can modify this look to suit more modest surroundings by concentrating on furnishings rather than features. Ornate mirrors, picture frames, chairs, bookcases, sideboards, and large dressers are all up for a dramatic transformation. This look is about grand gestures so keep things big—a pared-down interior with a few large, good-looking pieces will work, but filling the place with a lot of brightly colored small and undistinguished pieces won't. This look is perfect if you have antique furniture, which will look great against these colors; polished wood furniture and floors provide welcome respite from so much excitement.

There is no need for fancy furniture if it is not to your taste, though; just use the colors in a simpler way as part of a dark, rich color scheme. Paint the walls in a dark, restrained color such as plum, and use the bright purples, brilliant greens and turquoises sparingly but effectively.

Opposite: This highly polished collection of old kitchen utensils and household items adds an authentic glow to this richly colored interior.

DRAMATIC INTERVENTIONS

In a living room:
- Use a dark, subtly patterned wallpaper instead of paint
- Paint the floor deep purple
- Paint a set of French doors in bright green or turquoise
- Put up brilliantly colored damask drapes
- Use purple velvets and damasks for upholstery and cushions

In a hallway:
- Paint the front door with a deep turquoise glossy paint
- If you have beautiful wooden banisters, leave them alone; if not, paint them a brlliant jade green
- Paint the longest wall in bright purple, jade, or grass green

In a bedroom:
- Use purple velvets, silks, and damasks for bedcovers and cushions

- Line dark velvet Roman blinds with bright green or turquoise silk
- Cover a beautiful chair in an extravagant and colorful fabric

In a bathroom:
- Cover the walls in turquoise tiles
- Cover the walls in dark tiles and use brightly colored towels and accessories
- Paint the floor and/or bathtub panel in bright green or turquoise
- Paint the door and window frames in brilliant turquoise

In a kitchen:
- Paint old units bright green
- Paint window reveals or one wall bright turquoise
- Paint open shelves and dressers brilliant green
- Paint or cover the floor with a bright color to match the units

Above right: *The use of bright colors for the window, door frame, and even some of the beams transforms this kitchen from something old and traditional into something new and unexpected.*

Right: *The curvy shapes and unusual design of this fabulous doorway are emphasized by the choice of color and decoration, which may be new although it looks convincingly old.*

MAKE IT WORK FOR YOU

Vivid Scenes

This interior appears to break all the rules of taste and restraint but, though it looks like a cheerful hotchpotch, the choice and use of color is carefully controlled. There are three basic colors—blue, pink, and green, with smaller areas of flesh pink, deep pink, and splashes of red, shocking pink, and turquoise blue. The reason the color scheme appears quieter than it should is because the light green, pink, and blue are of similar strength, not too bright and with quite a lot of white in them, and therefore don't compete for attention. Also, the floor has been painted in the same pink as the wall—a technique that is guaranteed to create a calmer impression. Of the three colors, the pink is slightly more dominant and for this reason has been confined mostly to the lower parts of the room with the fresher, pale green above to lighten things up. Pale blue, which is also used for some of the furniture, is a perfect antidote to pink and prevents it looking too sugary.

The main attraction of this scheme is that it is relaxed and, despite being part of a large high space, looks undeniably cozy. This is a cheap and easy look to emulate as it contains no expensive fittings and the assortment of furniture is mostly old.

Opposite: *Although several strong colors are used in this cheerful, quirky dining area, the pink, green, and pale blue are of similar character and strength, which ensures that the overall effect is surprisingly calm.*

COLOR PALETTE

Raspberry pink	Strawberry ice cream	Light blue	Light green	Bright blue
An intense color but its soft tones make it blend rather than shock. It can warm up cooler blues and greens and take the edge off sharp colors such as lime and shocking pink.	*A pale pink tint, a little darker than baby pink and consequently more grown up. On its own it can be a little too sugary so will benefit from being used with fresher colors.*	*A pale blue lightened with white rather than gray. Used on its own it can look cold and wishy-washy, but this fresh, clean color has an enlivening effect on other colors.*	*This green has similar properties to the light blue but, unlike the blue, can work well on its own with pink. It is a good color for kitchens and bathrooms.*	*This color can look harsh on its own, but here, where it is used in small amounts on the table legs and a single chair, it adds weight and contrast and stands out well against the pinks.*

Electric Shocks

Above: *The combination of curves, metallic finishes, and brilliant colors bring a touch of fantasy and movie-set glamour to this distinctive interior.*

At a time when old is the new "new," not everyone is in retreat and there are still people willing to embrace the 21st century and all it offers in the way of new materials, sleek design, and brilliant colors. We live in an almost super-colorful age, in which technology exposes us to new electronic, "virtual" colors that exist only by the presence of light. These electrically charged colors on computer and television screens and advertising hoardings may not exist in reality, but new materials and production methods have brought a new range of brilliant colors to the interior-design market. And if these are still not not sharp enough for your taste, then you can

always add extra zing in the form of clever lighting.

Synthetic materials are the obvious medium for these types of colors. New developments in paint production allow for more intense hues, and synthetic fabrics and dyes have brought about colors that never existed before. There is also a wide range of materials with metallic, highly polished, and high-gloss finishes, and a greater use of glass and acrylics in furniture, fixtures, and fittings.

Such materials and colours are naturally suited to a modern, space-age look, but brightly colored silks and velvets have their own luminosity, which can be used to light up a more traditional style of interior.

ELECTRICAL APPLIANCE

The intensity of these vibrant colors is best represented in high-tech, high-spec, innovative designs and materials. Even if you don't want to spend all day surrounded by luminous colors, sparkling finishes, high-gloss surfaces, and the latest technology, you may be more than happy to have them in your kitchen and bathroom.

Kitchens

Glass, metal, shiny surfaces and vibrant, dazzling colors are natural companions, which is why today's functional, sparkling kitchens are an obvious place to go electric. The effect of bright color will be multiplied by its reflection in glass or polished steel. Look out for tiles with metallic finishes and metal flooring, and think about having slatted metal shades in a bright color. Complete the circuit with shiny utensils, aluminum café furniture, glamorous steel-framed bars stools, and colored or transparent acrylic chairs—and lots and lots of light.

Bathrooms

You may prefer something a little more sober in the rest of your home but you can afford to be bold in the bathroom. Bathrooms are a good place to experiment as the solid shapes of white fittings stand out beautifully and provide light relief against bright colors. Also, in a small space, you can often afford to indulge in more expensive materials, especially when it comes to flooring. The sparkly nature of bathrooms is emphasized by shiny faucets and shower fittings, which reflect colors brilliantly, as do metallic or white glazed tiles, glass shower cubicles and shelving, chrome and stainless steel fixtures and fittings. For maximum impact, use electric colors for walls and bathtub panels as well as for towels and storage containers.

Above: *The ethereal blue seen in this interior can be created using lighting systems rather than paint, with which colors can be changed to suit different moods and requirements.*

Opposite: *The light coming in through the glazed wall illuminates the reflective surfaces of the floor and staircase to add extra brilliance to the colors.*

ELECTRICAL CURRENTS

The white box may not be cutting edge any more but the stark interior still has its appeal, only now it provides an opportunity to use brilliant, clear colors in a disciplined way that emphasizes clean lines and uncluttered spaces. Such interiors are suited to intense colors with more than a hint of electric blue, and while they may prove too cold and impersonal for many, for others they create an intentional ambience of cool efficiency.

This approach works very well in an open-plan interior, where different colors can be used to define different areas and functions or draw attention to particular details. Not everyone who loves modern, minimalist interiors is fortunate enough to live in a large, architect-designed house, but dramatic use of color is a perfect way to turn the mundane into the marvelous. It's all about straight lines, large areas of plain color, and lots of light.

This is a look that works best if it is applied throughout a whole house or apartment—and it is perfect for studio and live–work spaces. Painting a whole space in a light but bright aqua blue may sound extreme, but when one color is used on every surface, the effect is one of unity and therefore the impression is of calm rather than alarm.

Trick of the light

The way to make bright colors brilliant is to add light, and the way to create color where none exists is to add colored light. New developments in lighting allow you to create your own light show at home. Systems are available that change the colors in a room to suit different times of the day, different functions, and even different occupants. If you have the desire—and the means—it is possible to have a brilliantly colored space without using a drop of colored paint.

ILLUMINATING FACTS

If the high-tech option is out of your range, there are other ways in which you can illuminate your life and home.

● Wall washes direct light up and down a wall to add intensity to any color.

● The humble wall light performs a similar role, especially if you use several in a row rather than one or two. Use a row of bulkhead lights to light your way along a hallway, for example.

● Using concealed lighting under cupboards and shelving is a good way to illuminate brightly colored walls and objects.

● Lights set into the floor are no longer just for public spaces: they look great in a hallway or bathroom or set around the edge of the floor in a living area.

● When you don't need them for studying, aim desk lights at the wall. Simple but effective.

chalky

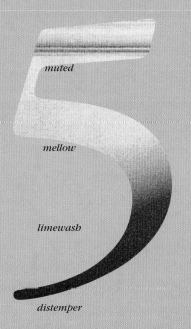

muted

mellow

limewash

distemper

HISTORICAL
Prussian blue

ASSOCIATIONS

yellow ocher

red ocher

chrome yellow

azure

Despite the fact that we live in a high-tech age, our interest in the past, especially in old houses, has never been greater. There is no doubt that older houses—not only the grand ones but also those of ordinary people—have a restful air about them redolent of a much simpler, and slower, pace of life, which appeals to those of us caught up in frenetic 21st-century lifestyles. The apparent tranquillity of these houses is to some degree due to the mellowing effects of age but also to the muted qualities of the colors used for decoration.

This interest has been picked up by paint manufacturers, resulting in the availability of several "historic" color ranges. Some of these manufacturers produce paint using traditional techniques and materials while others supply their versions of "old" colors in paints made with synthetic additives. The traditionally made paints normally contain more pigment and therefore the colors are more intense, but they are more expensive and more coats are often needed to get an even finish. Modern paints, on the other hand, are cheaper, cover well, and are easier to use.

Because there is so much interest in old houses, there is also a lot of information available on the colors used. This is especially useful for devotees of authenticity who wish to re-create the past, but you don't have to be a slave to history—or own a beautiful old house—to appreciate the subtlety and special qualities of the old colors. While it is often homes from the 18th and 19th centuries that attract much of the acclaim, other, more recent styles also have their enthusiasts. From the restraint of Modernism and Art Deco through to the exuberance of the fifties and sixties, each period and style has its own distinctive palettes and ways of using color.

Right: *This grand interior is treated in a simple but traditional way with the magnificent detailing picked out in gold, which glows beautifully in the romantic lighting.*

Traditional Ingredients

The so-called historic colors, especially those made from traditional ingredients, share similar characteristics, which make them appear softer and more subdued. This is because early paints were made without the synthetic whiteners and brighteners used in modern paints. Instead, they relied on

chalk, china clay, barium, and lead as lighteners, which gave them the grayish, slightly dirty look that we find so attractive today. Before the 18th century, the number of pigments readily available and affordable was mostly limited to umbers, siennas, and yellow ochers. Darker tones were achieved by heating these pigments. It was, therefore, often the lack of ingredients rather than inherent good taste that dictated the color schemes of the past that we so much admire today.

At one time, only the rich could afford strong colors. This is especially true of blue, which was made from expensive lapis lazuli. However, the development of Prussian blue, along with other newer and less expensive pigments, meant that stronger colors became more common, particularly during the early 19th century, when the discovery of chrome yellow not only provided a bright yellow but also influenced related colors such as blue.

The early 18th century saw the advent of Palladian architecture, which favored all-white interiors. Although there were plenty of stable red pigments around, red and pink were not fashionable until the mid-18th century. They became so again in early 19th century, when the availability of deeper, brighter reds coincided with the fashion for bright reds as discovered in the ruins of Pompeii and Herculaneum.

It is a mistake to think of historic colrs only in terms of the 18th and 19th centuries, however, as there are plenty that refer to movements and styles in the 20th century. The colours of the Art Deco era and the 1950s have their own distinctive colors and color combinations, and though we tend to associate the Modernists with white, they actually used a lot of bold colors.

Below left: *The muted coloring used on this paintwork is typical of the historical colors that would have been used when the house was built.*

Opposite: *This room could be in a modern home but a sense of history is suggested by the use of color as well as the old painting and antique sofa.*

Fine Finishes

The attraction of old paints lies not only in the colors but also in the finish, especially the chalky finish of the old distempers. Several paint manufacturers are producing paints that re-create the dense colors and the flat, matte surfaces used on both walls and paintwork. Colors vary according to the finish: in a high gloss, a color will look lighter than in a matte finish.

ORIGINAL RECIPES

Paints made according to old methods use natural products with pigments added to give the color. They normally contain a higher percentage of pigment than modern paints and so have a higher saturation of color. Despite this, more coats are normally needed in order to build up the color. One of the biggest advantages of these and other natural paints is that they are porous and therefore allow the wall to "breathe." Walls that cannot breathe are a major cause of damp problems in houses so these paints not only look good, they are also good for your home.

Limewash
One of the earliest types of paint, limewash is made from chalk and lime mixed with water. The surface is not very stable and rubs off easily so limewash is normally used only by purists.

Distemper

A similar mix to limewash but containing added binders in the form of glue and casein (milk solids) and sometimes a little linseed oil. This makes the surface more stable, and in some, the amount of chalk is reduced, which results in deeper colors. The big disadvantage of distemper is that you cannot paint over it with any other type of paint.

Shiny finishes

The addition of linseed oil creates a more robust and stable paint with a slightly glossy finish. A hard, durable surface was made possible by the addition of lead, which also had good covering power. Lead is a hazardous material and no longer used in paints, except for very special conservation projects; it has been replaced by safer alternatives such as titanium oxide.

Gloss finishes were often achieved with a separate coat of varnish until a paint with a hard shiny finish was made by adding varnish and omitting "matting agents." Some of these oil-based paints require several coats to build up the depth of color and a hard surface, and in order to achieve a good finish, it is also necessary to sand down the surface between coats.

NEW RECIPES

Modern paints contain plasticizers, resins, and binders, which, as well as making the paints much easier to use, increase their covering power and allow for much brighter, cleaner colors. They are also less expensive than the so-called traditional paints. For ecological and safety reasons, most paints and primers are now water-based rather than oil or spirit-based.

Latex paint

Latex paint has replaced distemper and is much easier to use. It covers well and has a stable, hardwearing surface. This water-based paint is available in a huge range of colors and in matte or soft sheen finishes. It is also relatively inexpensive.

Eggshell

This paint gives a semimatte finish for paintwork. It has a slight sheen that is less shiny than gloss. It is perfect for the more understated look associated with older properties and historical paint techniques and effects.

Gloss

Obtaining a smooth, blemish-free, extra-shiny surface is becoming easier with modern, quick-drying gloss paints, which are formulated for ease of use.

Far left: The soft sheen finish used on the woodwork here is more appropriate to the style and age of this house than a hard gloss finish would be.

Below: The bold paint colors that have been used in this bathroom complement the equally strong character of the fittings and the beautiful tiled floor.

Historically Correct

When we think of historic colors, it is usually the soft muted hues that come to mind, but although they lack the brilliance made possible with new paints, the darker shades in these ranges are no less dramatic.

Red

Deep tones are produced with pigments such as red ocher and yellow ocher, which can be burned to produce even darker shades. These earth pigments would have formed the basis of the deep, warm, earthy red found in the ruins of Pompeii and Herculaneum. As the basis of terra-cottas and pinks, these tones have long been a staple color in Mediterranean countries, but they also appear in grand country houses and even Modernist masterpieces. These warm earthy reds work well with deep blue.

Pigments such as vermilion and carmine produce more intense, pure reds, which look equally at home in traditional or modern settings. They also look stunning in a gloss finish.

Cobalt blue

The addition of cobalt creates an intense pure blue familiar from old blue and white china. In a chalky matte finish it recedes and looks darker but in a shiny finish it glows brighter. This is a powerful, dominating color and works well with white though it can also look sensational with bright yellow.

Pea green

The color of young or frozen peas rather than the more muted tones of pea soup. A deep color, which is also clean and clear, this is very versatile in that it can look fresh and modest in simple surroundings or grown-up and sophisticated, especially with gold.

Forest green

A very dark green that is not too somber as it still has some yellow in it. Forest green can be too overwhelming in large quantities but is a good color to use if you want contrast without too much drama.

Yellow ocher

Because it is based on the earth pigment, this essentially mellow yellow has warmth rather than brilliance. It has a calming effect on other colors but, thanks to its gentler qualities, stands up well on its own, too, even in large quantities. Old ochers complement old houses but get a new lease of life as hot mustard in contemporary settings.

Chrome yellow

The discovery of chrome yellow led to much brighter shades of yellow that were cooler and lighter than the ochers. Chrome yellow is equally at home as the star of an elegant dining room complete with silk furnishings or in a cheerful modern interior teamed with bright red or blue.

MAKE IT WORK FOR YOU

Historically Correct

Your bedroom may not be quite as impressive as this one but there are plenty of ideas that can be adapted for less distinctive homes. The atmosphere is serene even though five colors have been used, not including the colors in the printed panel. The colors on the walls and paneling are pale and understated and are the types of colors associated with elegant town houses and genteel lifestyles. This is quite an elaborate decoration scheme but the essential elements can be adapted to suit simpler surroundings and tastes.

Paneling was a feature of the grander houses of the 17th and 18th centuries where it was well suited to high ceilings and generous-sized rooms. It is relatively easy to create panels by fixing wooden moldings to a plain wall, but be careful or it could look rather tacky: use a generous wide molding and get the work done professionally. Alternatively, create "panels" in paint only: mark them out carefully and use masking tape to ensure a neat edge. In order to make rooms appear higher, make the panels tall and narrow. In a small room, especially if it has a low ceiling, restrict the number of panels, and if you have a lot of furniture, it might be a good idea to confine the paneling to one clear wall. Dark patterns can be overpowering in a small room so with printed panels, either limit their number or opt for a design with more muted colors.

Opposite: Despite the elaborate detailing and quite complex decorative scheme, this bedroom still retains an air of tranquil elegance.

COLOR PALETTE

Deep blue	**Pale apple green**	**Paler green**	**Warm pink**	**Pinky beige**
A dark, deep color that is best used sparingly either as part of a pattern or in a luxurious fabric such as silk or velvet.	*This is a soft green, fresh enough to prevent the pink looking too sweet but pale and subtle enough to be used on paintwork.*	*A lighter, and slightly bluer, shade of the pale apple that is pale enough to look obviously different but not so light that it loses its green-ness.*	*A warm pink with added yellow and a small amount of gray to make it look subtle and sophisticated.*	*A darker shade of pink with added beige. It could look dull on its own but here it adds definition to the pale green and flesh pink.*

ADDED INGREDIENTS

Printed panel
A decorative panel provides a stark contrast to the low-key colors as well as introducing some pattern. These panels may well be fabric but printed wallpaper is an easier option.

Woodwork
You can paint attractive architraves, windows, baseboards, and paneled doors using three colors, as in the room illustrated here. If the room is small, stick to one or two colors only.

Moldings and cornices
If you are fortunate enough to have decorative moldings or cornices, paint them in a different color from the wall.

Furniture
If your room lacks distinguished features, introduce them in the form of furniture. Pick out the detailing on a closet with paneled doors, and add an ornate dressing table or bedhead, or a dresser with the drawer fronts painted a different color.

Old Character

Old houses often look more comfortable with their original peeling paintwork and patchy walls than they do when they are forced into a clean and tidy coat of paint. "Distressed" is no longer a polite euphemism for falling on hard times; instead, it has become a declaration of love and respect for the past life and historical credentials of a house. Those who have this respect would no more think of covering the walls of an old house than they would of painting over an original work of art because it didn't match the new color scheme.

If you are leaving the walls in all their faded glory, it is particularly important that you pay careful attention to the floor finish. As in any interior, a poor-quality or horrible floor can completely spoil the effect. Old or new solid wood floors work best with this look; laminates are not so good. Although bare floors will naturally complement this style, carpet can work too, especially the natural fibers such as seagrass and sisal. Oriental rugs and kilims are other obvious choices, as are large mats made from natural fibers and bound with cotton webbing. Modern rugs in plain or bold designs won't look out of place either.

Some people who have a natural affinity with this look can happily furnish a room with a battered and torn collection of furniture and artefacts and make it look wonderful, but for others, the look is more difficult to achieve, and there is a fine line between distressed and disastrous! It mustn't look simply as though you haven't bothered to decorate and neither is the style an excuse for neglect or scruffiness. As with most good interior schemes, discipline, tidiness, and cleanliness will help make it work.

The nature of old paintwork and walls means that though they are full of character, the colors are broken and undefined, so using a carefully thought-out color scheme will complement the beauty of the old surfaces and act as a focus against the muted background.

OLD FLATTERERS

White
One of the easiest ways to flatter these old interiors is with white; not a hard, blue-white but the soft white of unbleached cotton and linen. White upholstered chairs and sofas, especially if they are pretty shapes, look fabulous against an old wall. Off-white rugs and mats, shades, simple drapes, and white table linen or bed linen complete the picture. Choose thick cottons and linens or, if you want a grander look, self-striped fabrics and damasks.

Pink
Old plaster is normally either pink or gray so pink is a good choice for keeping the atmosphere warm and calm. Go for salmon pink with another deeper pink and add touches of burnt orange, muted red, and pale yellowy lime. For contrast, you could try dark gray. These earthy colors work beautifully in velvet and thick cottons as well as the cottons and wools of mats and kilims, where they are often used in combination.

Past and present
Sleek contemporary furniture looks fabulous in an old setting, but take care with the color. It may be tempting to use bright colors, but the pristine perfection of modern furniture is enough of a contrast so opt for strong, muted, historic colors such deep red, azure blue, emerald green, and golden yellow.

Opposite: *It takes courage to leave surfaces in their unfinished state, but here the distressed walls celebrate both the age of the building and the unusual curved ceiling.*

CHARACTER DEVELOPMENT

If you have a suitably distressed wall worth keeping, clean up the surfaces to get rid of loose paint, dust, and any obvious blobs of dirt, then seal the surface with wax or vanish. If there any large holes, simply fill them in—they will add to the character.

If, however, you have pristine walls but long for something more interesting, there are things you can do. Painting your own distressed surface is not easy, so unless you are skilled in the art department, either employ a professional or stick to something simpler.

Color washes

Putting color "washes" on a wall is a way of building an interesting surface that has a slightly uneven distribution of color. The technique involves using several coats of very thin, watered-down paint, so, depending on what colors you choose, paint the wall first in an ordinary latex paint. A white background is too stark, so choose a softer color: the muted grays and greens are good or use a pink that is close to the color of bare plaster.

These easy recipes use artists' paints as the base of the color wash. The water-based wash is easier to use than the glaze, but both methods produce results that are unpredictable, so be prepared to carry out lots of tests in an inconspicuous area before starting on the whole wall or room.

Wash

Add a good squeeze of artists' gouache or acrylic paint to a small amount of latex paint, add water, and mix thoroughly in order to avoid blotchiness. It is best if each coat is of the same strength, so measure out the amounts you use so that you can make further batches if necessary. Apply the wash using a large brush—it doesn't have to be applied evenly but it shouldn't be too patchy either so paint in large strokes across the wall. Each coat will show through to the next, creating an uneven, "distressed" look. Put on as many coats of paint as necessary to achieve the desired effect. Water-based washes should be sealed with varnish.

Glaze

This is a more ambitious project that will give a similar effect to a wash but with a glazed surface. As it involves the use of oil, it is more difficult to apply than a water-based wash and, consequently, the results may be more unpredictable.

Make up the glaze using one part commercial oil glaze to three parts of liquid solvent, plus one tablespoon of white undercoat or eggshell per every 1 pint. Add the tint in the form of artists' oil paint; the amount you use will depend on the depth of color you require. As with the wash, remember to measure out the color in order to get the right strength in further batches.

Left : The use of orange paint on the wall ties in the old, worn paintwork on the shutters to the cheerful floral print on the chairs.

Opposite: Even more character has been added to this room with trompe-l'oeil paint effects. The beautiful, subtle color scheme appears to have been inspired by the colors in the kilim.

Old Color, New Look

Historic colors don't have to be used in traditional ways; they are, after all, beautiful colors in their own right and therefore well worth using in modern settings too. The benefit of perusing historic paint charts is that they will provide you with an edited selection of colors that share similar qualities and which therefore, on the whole, naturally work well with one another. This is particularly true of the traditionally made paints, whose similar tones derive from the fact that they are all made from the same base of natural ingredients and pigments.

In modern buildings, architects and interior designers have started using much more color than they did in the past. This is partly because many materials are now available in better and more sophisticated colors than ever before, but also because there is more of an appetite for color among consumers. Modern design is often associated with bright intense colors but many designers also appreciate the depth of color, muted tones, and matte finishes that are associated with the historic paints. The dark colors, in particular, have great strength but also great subtlety, unlike modern, brilliant colors, which tend to make their presence felt in a loud way.

These old colors and paints are also much kinder to modern homes, which often have little character and no distinguishing features. In addition, new paints, which contain less pigment and therefore have a less dense color, are made using synthetics, which produce an even finish that can be unforgiving and more likely to highlight imperfections. The soft chalky colors and textures of old-fashioned paints smooth over the rough edges and create a gentler ambience.

Opposite: *Whatever the style and age of a house, using old-style paints and colors can create an atmosphere that is subdued without being in any way gloomy.*

Right: *Pink is not an easy color to use on walls, but here it is freshened up with pale green, turquoise, and white to create a look that is grown-up and sophisticated.*

rubies

emeralds

amber

tapestries

medieval

RICH TAPESTRY

old masters

Persian rugs

kilims

candlelight

Surrounding yourself with the comfort of textiles, textures, and pattern is the perfect antidote to clean, minimal living. It's a look that many would consider old-fashioned, but in fact it's beyond fashion, a style that has existed in slightly different forms for hundreds of years. In grand stately homes, the wall hangings and drapery are an affirmation of the wealth of the owner as much as of good taste, as well as evidence of patronage and travel.

However, the rich tapestry of life is also to be found in more modest surroundings such as cozy parlors, where pattern creates a friendly habitat for warm relations and tea and sympathy. In traveler's trailers, lack of space is no deterrent to turning the interior into a veritable patchwork quilt of treasured possessions. The patterns of Asia and of Africa never go out of fashion and their influence can be seen in both old and contemporary textiles. Floral patterns, too, are always popular in some form, whether spriggy prints or big splodgy flower shapes and geometric plant life.

How you use your pattern permit is up to you. If you choose to leave no surface uncovered, swathing furniture in rugs and throws and floors with kilims and Persian rugs, that's fine. If you favor a more restrained use of pattern, then add richness with color. However, while a joyful jumble of colored patterns can work for some people, not everyone can do it. If you're in doubt, keep a color theme running through the different designs and use pattern in specific places, leaving areas of plain color to give them a chance to breathe and to stand out. Use what you have and what you like, and don't be afraid to put together your own personal style. It could even reawaken an interest in sewing and knitting—a huge wall hanging may be out of your league, but you could start with some needlepoint cushion covers.

Right: *The tapestry wall hanging completes the picture and adds to the aura of richness and texture in this opulent room.*

Passion for Pattern

Above: *An old railroad passenger car offers an unusual space emphasized by a bold color scheme, which is nevertheless limited to shades of green and red.*

Opposite: *There is a joyful feel to this interior full of obviously much-loved things. Nevertheless, as above, the colors here mostly conform to a deceptively disciplined palette.*

It's good to be able to use patterns again without incurring the wrath of the style police and the anticlutter detectives, and a relief to eschew the plain and simple and the pared down in favor of something a little more decorative and even busy. Whether you go for classic or retro, floral or geometric, ethnic or Asian, there is no shortage of fabrics, wallpapers, carpets, ceramics, and accessories to tempt you back to pattern. You could even reinstate the chintz!

Putting pattern center stage needs a bit of careful direction, however. The difficulty lies not so much in making it look good than in avoiding it appearing too considered—the days of mix-and-match coordinates are over, but with so many different types of design and colors to choose from, it can be difficult to create organized chaos rather than a disorganized mess.

Print works

A fresh way of using prints is to choose those with dark or colored backgrounds and set them in a bright, bold setting that is more gypsy trailer than country cottage, and more French Provençal than toiles de Jouy. If you deliberately choose patterns that contain little or no white, the colors will appear more solid and therefore more dramatic.

Flower power

Rather like a wild, unkempt backyard, a mixture of different floral fabrics somehow works. It does help if they have some colors in common, but if not, you can link them by picking out some of their main colors and using them as plain fabrics or paint colors. Try to have a mix of large and small patterns and opt for dark backgrounds.

Retro heaven

The patterns from a specific era will all share a similar look, not only because of the designs and colors but also because of the types of dyes and fabrics used. The popular patterns of the fifties are gloriously colorful and love to be part of a crowd. Although they enjoy the company of furniture and artefacts from the same era, they are equally happy with other styles.

Pattern pending

Not everyone wants or likes an excess of pattern or decoration, and those who favor the more pared-down, modern approach may prefer their patterns to be kept under control. However, it is possible to invoke rich tapestry with color, texture, and a few well-chosen extras. Try richly colored walls, sleek furniture in plain-colored textured fabrics and a single beautiful rug hung on the wall, for example.

MAKE IT WORK FOR YOU

Passion for Pattern

If you are looking for an opportunity to indulge your passion for prints then the ideal place to start is a bedroom. This cozy niche is prevented from being quaint by the use of deep, warm red paint and a dark print. The fact that the colors make the place feel small is of no consequence—its smallness is its biggest feature.

The printed dado is an unusual touch that adds to the quirkiness. The choice of a dark-colored print balances the color of the wall above and prevents things looking top heavy. For a really cozy effect, the dado has become an extended padded headboard made from fabric, but a printed wallpaper could give a similar effect.

There is an orderliness in this neat sleeping area that gives the impression that there is a place for everything and everything is in its place. The bed is covered with an eclectic collection of fabrics and quilts in which the color theme is predominantly dark or at least quiet. The cushions are neatly arranged, and even the assemblage of pictures, pretty shelves, and objects fixed to the wall look organized. The plain, functional shelves are painted the same color as the walls and so stay in the background. The jolly, patterned containers also share a similar style and coloring.

Opposite: The use of predominantly dark colors, especially on the walls, ensures that the overall impression is dramatic rather than pretty.

COLOR PALETTE

Deep red	Bright red	Deep turquoise	Pink
An intense, warm yet muted color that is relaxing rather than stimulating. Because it is an earthy color, this deep red goes with almost any other color and won't dominate.	*This bright red can be found in all types of design and patterns. It is therefore a useful color to use in bringing together a diverse collection of prints and patterns.*	*A rich, deep color that is nevertheless bright and cheerful. With the red, this color on its own would be too strong, but as part of a print that contains red it retains its power without overwhelming.*	*This clean, deep pink appears in several of the floral patterns here, where it provides a lighter, fresher alternative to bright or deep red.*

ADDED INGREDIENTS

Bedcovers
Pretty floral bed linen blends in with
the surroundings better than pure
white. Use a plain bedcover underneath
then add layers of fabric remnants,
tablecloths, old drapes, or patchwork
quilts. For other dark, bold patterns,
look at African prints, as well as Chinese
and Japanese fabrics, which often have
a lot of red and black in them.

Storage
Make pretty containers earn their place
and use them as useful storage. If you
need more space, you could have a
large trunk, either painted or covered
with patterned fabric. If closets and
dressers are spoiling the effect, paint
them to match the walls. If they look
too plain, stick printed paper on the
drawer and door fronts.

Extras
These delightful shelves and pictures
are the sort of things you find in
antique markets. If you have a more
disparate collection of objects, you
could paint some of them to bring
them together, but don't do everything
or it will look too self-conscious.

Dramatic dark interiors resemble these blackened oil paintings with their copious use of dark browns and almost blacks, and glimpses of brilliant colors in the form of fabric or perhaps paint. Dark interiors don't have to be gloomy: they can have an air of mystery or grandeur but still be surprisingly restful.

DARK INSPIRATIONS

Medieval hall

Imagine rooms hung with red tapestries and the comfort of roaring fires and pewter goblets filled with warm red wine. You can emulate the austerity of the baronial hall with plain, but beautiful furniture, wood and flagstone floors, patterned carpets, and wall hangings. Along with the colors of stone and dark polished wood, use the reds, greens, and blues of heraldry plus the earthy, muted tones of tapestries.

French château and English country house

If you like your dark a little more refined, the elegance of country houses and châteaux may be more to your taste. Lighten the dark with ornate furniture and chandeliers. Think of emerald-green and deep azure-blue silks and brocades set against a black background with flattering candlelight.

The souk

It is difficult to think of anywhere else that you will find such a plethora of elaborate patterns and rich colors, from the deep colorings of Oriental carpets to the browns, ochers, reds, and soft indigo of kilims. Yet despite their variety, they all share the subtle earthy quality characteristic of natural pigments. However, there are flashes of bright colors here too, and they provide the sort of contrast that makes the image of a pair of bright pink silk slippers on a Persian carpet such a pleasing one.

Old Masters

Above: *The beautiful silk damask glows wonderfully in this glorious, mainly golden, sumptuous interior.*

Opposite: *A white chair stands out beautifully against the dark, dramatic wallpaper, which, together with dark paintwork, brings an opulent, rich feel to this room.*

The masters of interior design have for centuries taken their inspiration from paintings. Some aim to capture the cool serenity of Vermeer's interiors, others are seduced by drapery or elaborate furnishings, and a few take their lead from still life. But all are influenced by the colors. Centuries ago, the pigments available to painters for mixing colors were limited to naturally occurring ones, most of which derive from the earth and so share an earthy quality. In addition, the varnishes used to protect the finished works contained oils that blacken over time, giving the paintings a somber, glistening appearance with only the brightest colors shining through.

DARK BROWN STUDY

Brown is a color often associated with gloomy old houses and dirt. It is also the disappointing color you got as a child when you mixed all those lovely bright colors together in your paintbox. Brown is often thought of as a dreary color, but like those small brown birds whose plumage appears boring at a distance, a closer look reveals an unimagined variety of subtle colorings that is anything but dull. Indeed, brown can be chic: cool gray-browns are a popular choice for modern furniture, where dark, heavily grained wood is fashionable, and smooth brown upholstery looks smart and sophisticated. Dark brown is the color of wood darkened with age, as well as of bitter and milk chocolate, rich loamy soil, and dry bracken.

Brown is also often considered to be gloomy, but as the ultimate earth color, it is close to nature and therefore a peaceful and relaxing color. However, too much brown can be depressing as well as dark. Unless you have huge, lofty rooms, it is best to confine brown to one wall or enjoy it as the rich, mellow tones of polished wood on floors, furniture, and even ceilings and walls.

Chocolate box

If you want to know what goes with delicious chocolate brown, imagine a box of chocolates decorated with bright pink, yellow, green, and violet sugar flowers. Then again, it looks good with white chocolate too!

Brown sugar

From raw to dark brown, from the golden shine of toffee and butterscotch to the softer matte of fudge, these sweeter browns are delicious, but you may need to add white elsewhere in the scheme to cleanse the palate.

A touch of brown

From buff to beige and bone to stone, these so-called "neutral" colors all contain a hint of brown, which gives them their warmth. The tiniest amount of added brown can turn white into cream and take the edge off red. Greige is a chic version of beige and contains brown and gray. It is a wonderfully understated color, as is taupe, which has an added touch of green. Undyed natural fibers also have a brownish tinge, which gives natural fabrics their muted appearance.

BROWNIE POINTS

Brown may be a strong color, but it is also versatile—you can change its mood depending on what colors you put with it.

- **Hot**
Yellow browns are a bit much—it is better to warm up a cooler brown with mustard, burnt orange, and chili red.

- **Mellow**
Chill out and watch those browns mellow with deep blushing pinks and golden yellows.

- **Cool**
Brown can look too warm and woolly. Sharpen it up with turquoise and lime green or smarten it up with pale aqua and pale blue.

Embarrassment of Riches

The owners of stately homes and country houses were certainly not embarrassed by their riches, and neither should you be. This is your opportunity to defy the light and airy brigade and surround yourself with the comfort of drapery and napery. Enjoy flowery wallpaper, layers of drapes, bits of lace, velvets, chenille, old carpets, and displays of pretty china. Go ahead and cover tables with cloths, drape old chairs with kilims, pile on the bedcovers, hang rugs on the wall—and if you were looking for an excuse to have swags and drapes, this could be it. The look may be reminiscent of a century ago, but it doesn't have to be old stuff—modern, simple shapes and clean lines are a good foil to prevent things getting out of hand. If you want ornament and pattern, there is plenty in the stores that is decorative. This is one time when an overly considered color scheme could spoil the effect. Go with your instincts, but avoid very bright colors—stick to the more muted shades, and enjoy!

RICH INGREDIENTS

Patterned wallpaper

The perfect opportunity to smother the walls in pattern, especially as there are now so many gorgeous designs on the market. Avoid white backgrounds, a lot of white, very wild colors, or very large designs. The Arts and Crafts' style has the right sort of richness of color and pattern, but there are also other designs inspired by bygone eras to choose from.

Oriental carpets

It's well known that these classic carpets will fit in with almost any style or color scheme. Threadbare is fine and layers are even better.

Treasured possessions

Minimalism has made us nervous of putting our possessions on display for fear of revealing our real character, but now is the time to get out the patterned china and finally put all those pictures on the wall. A wall of books will add color and texture.

Above: *This highly individual interior conforms to no specific style, but it does demonstrate the owners' passion for color, pattern, and textiles.*

Opposite: *The splendid wall hanging, together with the decorative table, ornamented chair, and harp, creates a wonderfully rich and rather theatrical setting.*

NOUVEAU RICHES

If you don't have trunks of old fabrics and draperies that have been waiting for a fashion moment to see the light of day again, you can always buy new versions, often very cheaply, at malls, markets, and the large furniture warehouses.

- **Curtaining**—as well as fabrics you can choose from a huge selection of ready-made and secondhand drapes plus window panels in lace and muslin.

- **Throws**—all kinds, from tartan and velvet to ethnic embroideries and patchwork.

- **Quilts**—not only as bedcovers, but also for walls, windows, sofas, and chairs.

- **Rugs**—plenty of kilims and dhurries, rag rugs, Oriental-style rugs and carpets, which, like quilts, also look good on chairs, sofas, beds, and walls.

Jewel Personality

Deep, rich colors with an inner glow bring to mind precious stones such as emeralds, rubies, sapphires, amethysts, and topaz, all with a common purpose—to dazzle and flatter. When choosing the contents of your own jewel box, make sure your jewels have the beauty and depth of the real thing rather than the more brash sparkle of costume jewelry. Genuine stones can be mixed together without looking vulgar as their quality always shines through.

JEWEL BOX

Amethyst, ruby, and garnet

Royal purples and regal reds look grand and expensive, especially in velvets, silks, and damasks, and are perfect for an elegant and grown-up living room, dining room, or bedroom. The deeper colors have a natural air of sobriety,

which makes them suitable for places where relaxation is the main activity. Colors at the purple end of the spectrum need to look expensive, so make sure they are not too harsh and cheap looking. To avoid things becoming too overpowering, keep furnishings simple and introduce lighter colors such as pale amethyst, citrine, and aquamarine. To spark things up a bit, introduce some diamond brightness with glass and clear acrylic furniture, crystal chandeliers, and white linens.

Topaz and amber

These soft, mellow colors are gentler and lend themselves to elegant settings with touches of gold. They will glow in silks and damask wallpapers but look ethnic and earthy in coarse linens and chunky wool. If the look gets a bit heavy and syrupy, freshen it up with silver and aquamarine. If you want something hotter, add garnets and dark amethyst.

Sapphire, aquamarine, and turquoise

Blue colors have a reputation for being cool, but cool also implies chic and elegant. These colors suit an 18th-century town house style and look wonderful with silver and diamond crystal, but they can also be lively, and bring a splash of brilliance to modern interiors, where they sparkle with shiny metal. In their paler forms, they have a low-key serenity and freshness.

Jade and emerald

The nature of these greens gives them depth and variation, which is why they look good in velvet and silk. Because they are quite dark and powerful, they are better in a supporting role than as the main attraction. Use with amethysts, rubies, garnets, and gold, and brighten them up with citrines and diamonds.

Below left: *These magnificent, emerald silk embroidered drapes glow like jewels in their dark, richly furnished environment.*

Opposite: *The unusual light source, which resembles an illuminated pearl necklace, throws out just enough light to turn the beads on the floaty fabric into twinkling jewels.*

MAKE IT WORK FOR YOU

Jewel Personality

Though your home may not be as grand as this one, it is possible to create a jewel box ambience in even the most prosaic room by using a relatively small palette and carefully chosen accessories. There is a lot of color in this room yet the overall impression is of serenity. A strong green is the background to a richly patterned wallpaper and so shares some of its glory with the floral pattern, and its light-reflecting sheen softens the color. Green is tempered by touches of ruby red, a color scheme also echoed in the carpet, and gold. The paintwork is a pale color rather than white (which would look too stark) and the wooden floor has a mellowing effect. The room is not cluttered and the floor cushions and table keep a low profile so as not to confuse the eye or detract from the stunning wallpaper. The cushions are a softer green and act as a foil to the brilliance of the walls and help to create a sense of calm. For best effect, keep to a relatively small palette of colors, paint the woodwork in a paler version of the color rather than white, choose colors that blend with the main color rather than contrast, and avoid overcrowding the room.

Opposite: The light from the fire and candles adds the final sparkling jewel touch to this room, but even without it, the colors of the furnishings and wallpaper will retain a warm glow.

COLOR PALETTE

Emerald	**Moss green**	**Pale green**	**Ruby**	**Gold**
Strong greens can dominate a room and also make it look dark, so when choosing paint, think about using a soft sheen or eggshell, or a slightly paler version if you want a matte finish.	*The softer, grayer tones of mossy greens will help tone down any brash tendencies of sparkling emerald, and the paler shades are perfect for paintwork.*	*Pale greens that contain a hint of gray look subtle and sophisticated, especially when used in an eggshell finish. Using them as an alternative to white on the woodwork will help to bring a sense of calm to a room.*	*Red and green can be difficult together but here their jewel-like quality unites and harmonizes. Red will warm up green but use it sparingly so that it complements rather than competes for attention.*	*Jewels are set in gold for the good reason that it highlights them beautifully, which is why gilt-framed mirrors and pictures work so well. Gold in fabric form is effective too, but think topaz and amber rather than yellow.*

ADDED INGREDIENTS

Wallpaper
A heavily patterned wallpaper all over a
small room can look sensational as long
as you allow it to take center stage and
keep everything else under control. An
alternative is to paper just one wall and
paint the rest in a softer shade of the
dominant color in the wallpaper.

Mirrors
As well as adding to the overall
richness of a room, a gilt-framed mirror
will make the space feel larger and will
double the power of the lighting.

Oriental carpets
Despite their elaborate patterns and rich
colorings, Oriental carpets seem to go
with anything. Old ones are the best as
the dyes used are natural and have a
mellower tone.

Flattering light
Throughout history, jewels have always
responded well to candlelight and
firelight, which also impart a flattering
and romantic glow to a jewel-inspired
interior. A chandelier adds grandeur as
well as a gentler form of light.

Asian Opulence

You don't have to travel extensively to bring Asian opulence to your home; there are plenty of treasure chests waiting to be plundered in stores and antique emporia throughout the land. Choose from the sumptuous embroideries of India, the brilliant colors of Thailand, and the elaborate patterned silks of China. Many of the colors are gloriously gaudy and guaranteed to cheer up any room.

This is an opportunity to adopt a different way of working with color, by using artefacts rather than color charts as your source and guide. Whether you adopt a "go-for-it" attitude or a more considered approach will depend on your personal taste and pattern tolerance threshold, but whether you opt for a riot or an orderly gathering, it is sure to be an enriching experience.

Asian excess

Decorative artefacts of diverse styles and from various parts of the world often share an exuberance and artlessness that enables them to overcome their differences and work together in a sort of chaotic harmony. You might get away with a jolly jumble of prints, embroideries, decorative furniture, and artefacts, but to create a medley rather than a mess, it is wise to place things in groups rather than at random, and to mix in some plain colors too. Too many garish colors could be uneasy on the eye, so make sure you include some of the subtler tones. Don't allow special or more beautiful items to get lost in the crowd; give them space to breathe and the attention they deserve.

Transcendental meditation

Opulence doesn't have to involve excess. If you prefer a more Zen approach to Asia, choose just a few items or colors and make them the focus of attention in a simpler, more pared-down scheme.

This style is particularly suited to traditional Chinese black and red lacquered furniture and accessories, which should be used in a minimal way and look best when arranged in ordered fashion according to tradition, and perhaps the rules of feng shui. An impression of opulence can be created with a single swathe of brilliant red silk, or suggested by a pile of richly colored, embroidered cushions. A more subtle, though no less opulent ambience is possible with more subdued colorings, as in a room filled with old and faded furniture, furnishings, carpets, and wall hangings.

Opposite: *Whatever size or style of room, this brilliant red embroidered silk and charming lacquered table is sure to create an ambience of exotic opulence.*

Below: *Asia provides a rich source of treasures. Sometimes just one is enough to provide the inspiration for a whole interior.*

chalks

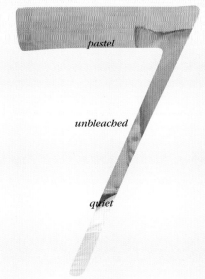

pastel

unbleached

quiet

Morandi

PALE AND
alabaster

INTERESTING

driftwood

natural

restful

With the pace of life showing no obvious signs of slowing down, our homes have often become a sanctuary, a place to relax, unwind, and restore our equilibrium. The restorative qualities of an interior will be enhanced if the ambience is one of calm simplicity with as few distractions as possible, and it goes without saying that an interior that is pale and interesting will be more restful than one that is a riot of color.

One of the best things about many of the new paint, fabric, and wallpaper ranges is the variety and subtlety of the lighter colors, which can be used successfully in a color scheme suitable for any style or mood, whether in a country cottage, an elegant house, or a strikingly modern interior. Subtle, pale colors soften spaces and are kind to your home, and unlike pure white, which can highlight imperfections, slightly darker tones can play them down and make them less conspicuous. They are also more respectful of distinctive architecture and features and will take the hard edges off new properties.

Soft, muted colors help to create a wonderfully harmonious atmosphere, which, though it may not be as light as with white, is nevertheless very calm and restful. However, pale isn't necessarily all about serenity: it can also be smart and crisp. Some of the paler, grungier colors are extremely fashionable and can look cool and sophisticated when used in conjunction with modern furnishings in a pared-down interior.

The options for making pale interesting include a monochrome approach, using one color only plus shades and tones of it, or a more colorful style, where several colors of similar quality and strength are used to create a slightly livelier atmosphere that is neverthless refreshingly calming.

Opposite: Painting a witty trompe-l'oeil mural is a good way to make an otherwise minimal interior appear more human and less severe.

Spatial Harmony

It is a well known decorating fact that painting a whole house or collection of rooms in one color will unify the space as well as making it feel more spacious. White, or white with a hint of something, has traditionally been the unifying color of choice, but while white does the job quite efficiently, it can sometimes look too stark, especially in older properties. These days, fortunately, there is a much wider and more interesting selection of pale colors from which you can choose to create harmonious interiors.

Opting for a monochrome scheme means using just one color, but this is not as restrictive as it sounds as the palette also contains all the tints, tones, and shades of that color, thus providing plenty of scope for a color scheme that is harmonious without being monotonous. One of the benefits of new paint colors is that there are now many more gradations within each color, making it easier to choose and use a monochrome palette.

Texture and finish also provide tonal variety. Paintwork in gloss or eggshell will look paler than a matte wall in the same color, and textiles in similar colors but different textures will also add light and shade.

Incorporating floors and furnishings into a monochrome theme will ensure a thoroughly restrained ambience, but if you want a little more variety, you can add other colors that are similar in tone and quality to the main color. Being disciplined in your color scheme doesn't mean that you need to be a minimalist capable of maintaining a completely clutter-free zone—the monochrome look can cope with a comfortable amount of stuff, though it will help if objects on display also comply with the color theme.

LIGHT TOUCH

To complete the pale and interesting picture, it is important that your furnishings blend in and don't spoil the atmosphere. White is an obvious choice, with unbleached cottons and linens for upholstery, plain white cotton or wool rugs, white drapes and shades, and white-painted furniture. If white looks too stark, you could use the very palest versions of the chosen color. Alternatively, if you want textural relief, stripped or unpainted wood works well.

Opposite, top: *While white can look stark and cold, adding just a hint of blue, as here, will give an interior a gentler feel and a more interesting ambience.*

Opposite, bottom: *With so many doors and so much glass, this space could seem cold and inhospitable, but the use of a pale tint and a matte finish brings unity and an air of serenity to the space.*

Above: *The use of one basic color throughout keeps things simple here. Even the objects on the unusual, ornate dresser conform to a strict color code.*

The New Pastels

There was a time when pastel shades were mostly limited to pale blue, baby pink, primrose yellow, and lilac—the colors of sugared almonds, and a little too sweet for modern tastes. Whereas the old pastels were often confined to nurseries and children's rooms, new pastels are suitable for adult use throughout the whole house. These new colors are more intense, and whereas the old versions were whitened variants of darker colors, the new ones are more complex and therefore much more subtle. They are more like artists' oil pastels, which contain quite a lot of pigment and produce a dense matte finish. Among these new pastels are pale ochers, dusty pinks, chalky blues, khaki greens, and dove grays.

One advantage of the new pastels is that, providing you choose those with a similar quality and color saturation, you can use several together without upsetting the balance, allowing you to create different atmospheres and color schemes that suit different settings as well as the varying personal tastes of others who share your home. Although they are essentially pale, the colors nevertheless have character, so that even those who want to upset the balance with a more lively color scheme may be persuaded to accept something more subtle. Little girls may want sugar pink in their bedrooms but might settle for dusty or "ointment" pink, and most boys would appreciate grungy, "dirty" green.

Opposite: The muted, grayish tones shown here typify the new pastel shades, which look soft yet sophisticated. Here, they complement beautifully the decorative detailing on the closet and mirror.

TONED DOWN

There are lots of ways to use several muted tones together to create something that is colorful yet quiet.

- Rather than using white or a paler version of the main color, paint windows, doors, baseboards, and floors a different color from the walls.

- If your woodwork is not up to much, paint it the same color as the walls and add interest in the form of a border of a different color around a door or a window. Ensure that it is quite wide so that it makes a bold statement.

- Large expanses of wall, such as in a hall or on a staircase, often have a dado complete with dado rail, which is the perfect excuse to use two different colors. Put the "heavier" color below and the lighter one above. If you don't have a dado, you can create one with paint.

- Stencils have had a bad press, but if you use colors that are very similar they turn from quaint into something sophisticated. Don't dot them around, though, and instead of applying them as borders, use large designs such as huge bunches of flowers, or cover the wall in an all-over damask or geometric pattern.

- Painted furniture looks great in the new pastel colors, which are not only perfect for old furniture but also soften the edges and add character to new pieces.

Raw Materials

The high-tech, high-spec, fast-moving world we now live in has left many people longing for a less complicated way of life. Unfortunately, for most of us, the simple life is just not a realistic option; nevertheless, our homes can offer peace and respite in the form of clutter-free, peaceful interiors created using natural materials.

An affinity with nature is often associated with well-being, and the use of natural materials in the home can indeed create a particularly harmonious atmosphere. Such materials will inevitably share certain qualities, and many have a gentle, subtle coloration that is enhanced by textures and the nonuniformity that is found, for example, in wood grain and the natural imperfections of stone. While some stones, such as granite and slate, have dark colorings, most have a mellow appearance.

By using natural materials in their raw state we can appreciate their qualities even more and their presence helps to create a back-to-nature feel, which many find relaxing and restorative. This simplicity is redolent of Zen-inspired interiors, where there are no extraneous objects to distract the mind. Such spaces suggest austerity, yet appear, and feel, restful rather than bleak.

Left: *Natural materials have an inherent beauty, as can be seen in the textures, colors, and raw qualities of the stone and wood used in this very simple washroom.*

Opposite: *The rough, characterful brickwork gives a rustic, utilitarian look to this unusual kitchen, which is enhanced by the industrial-sized sink and basic fittings.*

RAW INGREDIENTS

Natural fibers
The choice of materials is wide: think about cottons and linens for upholstery and drapes, simple window panels and shades, while for floors, you could use rush matting, seagrass, sisal, jute, coconut-fiber matting, or even paper.

Wool
Creamy, unbleached wool fabrics are great for upholstery, curtaining, and throws, and wool is an obvious option for floors, too, in the form of chunky woven mats and tufted woollen rugs and carpets.

Linoleum and rubber
Both linoleum and rubber are made from natural ingredients, and both have a warmth and offer endless possibilities for color and design.

Willow, rattan, and bamboo
These tough grasses provide a lighter alternative to wood for chairs, tables, footstools, ottomans, and shelving, not to mention accessories such baskets, mats, and bamboo shades.

Stone
There are numerous types to choose from, including limestone, slate, shiny marble, and granite. Stone is good not only for floors but also for sinks and bathtubs, backsplashes, and surrounds. The main ingredient of ceramic tiles is clay so they are another natural alternative for floors and walls.

Wood
Wood is one of the most ubiquitous and versatile natural materials and has intrinsically beautiful properties. Make the most of its mellow presence in floors, furniture, and slatted wooden shades as well as in structural features such as beams, staircases, windows, doors, architraves, and baseboards.

Faded Elegance

The passion for "shabby chic" has proved to be more than just a passing fashion whim, and the battered chair, peeling paintwork, and faded fabrics still exert their charm. The patinated surfaces and faded colors associated with old furnishings and interiors work well in a noncompetitive, nonintrusive environment, which is why pale, muted colors provide the perfect background.

If you have an old property with its own built-in character, a subdued color scheme will complement the features and allow them to stand out. But faded elegance is not restricted to old houses: it can be created in new or less elegant surroundings with old furniture and furnishings, which will also show up best against light colors. Neither are modern furniture and furnishings incompatible with old and elegant. On the contrary, they can provide a wonderfully fresh contrast against distressed walls and paintwork, well-worn floors and carpets, and can sit happily among other more ornate furniture and decorative items such as mirrors, chandeliers, and pictures.

AGING GRACEFULLY

Furniture

Now that signs of age are a selling point, old furniture has become expensive, but it is quite easy to create an impression of age with simple paint techniques. After painting, imitate signs of wear by rubbing off some of the paint along the edges. For a softer finish, paint furniture with latex paint and then give it a sheen with a coat of beeswax, which will also darken the color slightly.

Floors

Bare wooden floors finished with oil and wax are perfect evidence of faded elegance. If you need a new floor but an old look, buy recycled wood from salvage yards or specialist outlets. Alternatively, paint floorboards with latex paint and finish with wax or matte varnish—they will quickly develop their own patina of age. Another option is to apply a limed finish, which gives wood a white-washed appearance. Liming kits are widely available from home improvement stores.

Opposite: *Signs of age such as old paintwork and finishes somehow add elegance and create the impression of a house comfortable in its skin.*

Above: *The neutral palette ensures that nothing disturbs the calm of this room or detracts from the architecture or the antique furniture.*

Right: *A coat of pale paint looks fresh and forms the perfect backdrop here to the scrubbed wooden table and the old paint finishes on the chairs and glass-fronted unit.*

Gentle Tones

Right: *The clean lines of this modern interior are emphasized by the use of harmonizing neutral colors and natural materials to create a warm ambience.*

Pale, creamy whites, warm grays, and cool beiges are associated with modern, sleek furniture and smooth surfaces, but whereas once the preferred color for the surroundings would have been white, now you are likely to find other, subtler tones, which soften the atmosphere.

Old white is the new white

Many of the new paint colors, particularly in the historic ranges, are described as white, yet appear not to be white at all. This is because, as we've already seen, it is modern ingredients that make modern paints so white. Old paints were based on lime and chalk, which produced much dirtier colors. These "old" whites are tinged with varying amounts of green, beige, blue, and ocher, which means that some are warm while others are cool.

When these whites were originally developed, they were used in expansive spaces such as large country houses, where they do give an overall impression of white. Now, they provide a chic alternative to pure white and work very well in ultramodern settings. It can be difficult to see from a small sample just how dark or light, warm or cool these colors are. As they can be surprisingly colorful in certain situations, it is a good idea to buy sample pots and try them out before choosing.

Look sharp

If all this relaxation and serenity gets a bit too much, you can sharpen up subtle shades and restrained interiors with smooth, shiny finishes and uncompromisingly contemporary designs. If you feel the need to add refreshing colors, try ice blue and lemon yellow. If you prefer your living and sleeping spaces to be relaxing, confine the wake-up call to kitchens and bathrooms.

SMOOTH FINISHES

- **Gloss paint**—give a gleam to the pale colors or provide a contrast with brilliant white paintwork.

- **Glazed wall tiles**—for a change, use buff tiles in a bathroom: they give white fittings an extra sparkle.

- **Polished limestone**—use for walls, sinks, bathtubs, counters, and surrounds as well as for floors.

- **Ceramic floor tiles**—an alternative to stone to give your home a crisp, cutting-edge feel.

MAKE IT WORK FOR YOU

Gentle Tones

There is a wonderful air of serenity in this room that is created by the very restrained, very disciplined color scheme. Apart from the green walls and touches of gold in the wall light and chair, everything else is a shade of white, but the overall effect is much richer than would be expected with such a small palette. The combination of the old paint and decorative detailing on the cabinet, plus the the unusual collection of objects on the table, provides a huge number of variations on a theme of off-white, and the gilt on the chairs, wall light, and curtain pole and finial add warm support to the scheme. There is nothing new, or brightly colored, to disturb this scene, yet despite the fact that all the contents are obviously old, the careful arrangements and use of color make the room look quite fresh and contemporary. You don't have to have antique furniture or an old property to create this look; it can work just as well with the clean lines of modern furniture and accessories, as long as you restrict the palette to a background color plus off-white or cream and the mellowing tones of wood.

Opposite: The furniture and magnificent corals are the center of attention in this room, which looks calm and uncluttered despite the collections of beautiful objects.

COLOR PALETTE

Soft green	Off-white	Gilt	Pale khaki
This muted green relates to the greeny-tinged gilt on the chair and curtain pole and finial. Although it doesn't impose itself, it provides a dark enough background to allow the furniture and objects to stand out.	*In this situation, off-white is a loose term used to describe a number of shades that are in many ways indefinable—their subtlety is provided by aging, texture, and nature rather than by pigments.*	*The patina of gilt gives it a warm, greenish tinge, which harmonizes with the wall color and blends in with the general feeling of things that have a past.*	*A soft, warm color—not quite brown and not quite green—this pale khaki will change its appearance depending on the other colors used with it as well as in different lights.*

ADDED INGREDIENTS

Furniture
The beautiful cabinet is ornate, yet more rustic than grand, and a plainer, glass-fronted bookcase could work as well. Mixing old and new and different styles makes a more interesting, individual interior. Look for small, unusual chairs in antique markets and flea markets, and rather than a solid upholstered chair, go for an older, more elegant style.

Accessories
Chandeliers and wall lights give a softer, more romantic light and can be used in a variety of settings, including the very modern. They work best used as a witty addition rather than a centerpiece.

Beautiful objects
The objects in this collection are small in number but big on impact, thanks to their large sizes and wonderful shapes.

- **Character:** soft, muted, elegant, and understated

- **Colors:** mole, elephant, chinchilla, mouse, dove

- **Materials:** velvet, wool, silk, cashmere, gray flannel, carpeting

- **Freshen up with:** white, pale aqua, pale blue, turquoise, and chrome yellow

- **Added warmth:** deep pink, burnt orange, deep red, dark brown

COOL GRAYS

- **Character:** cool, hard-edged, sharp, functional

- **Colors:** steel, battleship gray, slate gray, granite

- **Materials:** stainless steel, aluminum, galvanized steel, zinc, slate, granite

- **Warm up with:** ochers, oranges, warm reds, deep pink

- **Cool it with:** white, aqua, blue

Gray Area

Above: *In this bathroom, the gray metallic finishes look crisp and efficient, as well as being a practical choice, and the filing cabinet is a perfect, and useful, addition.*

Opposite:
A roaring fire banishes any coldness associated with concrete, as do the soft, warm gray walls, which also harmonize with the subtle tones of the painting.

Gray is a color that can look gorgeously sophisticated or desperately dull depending on how it is used. Though pure gray is a mixture of black and white, most versions also contain varying amounts of blue, red, yellow, and green to produce a range of colors that can be both striking and subtle. Gray suggests vagueness, and while it could be described as a neutral color— pale grays are good background colors—it can also be a dominant presence in its darker forms.

Although gray goes with almost any other color, it also has definite cold and warm identites. Warm versions of gray veer toward pink and sometimes need waking up with a cleaner, sharper color. Cooler versions contain blue and green, and while their coolness can be asset, especially in a bathroom or kitchen, in other situations, cool grays respond well to the addition of warm or even hot colors.

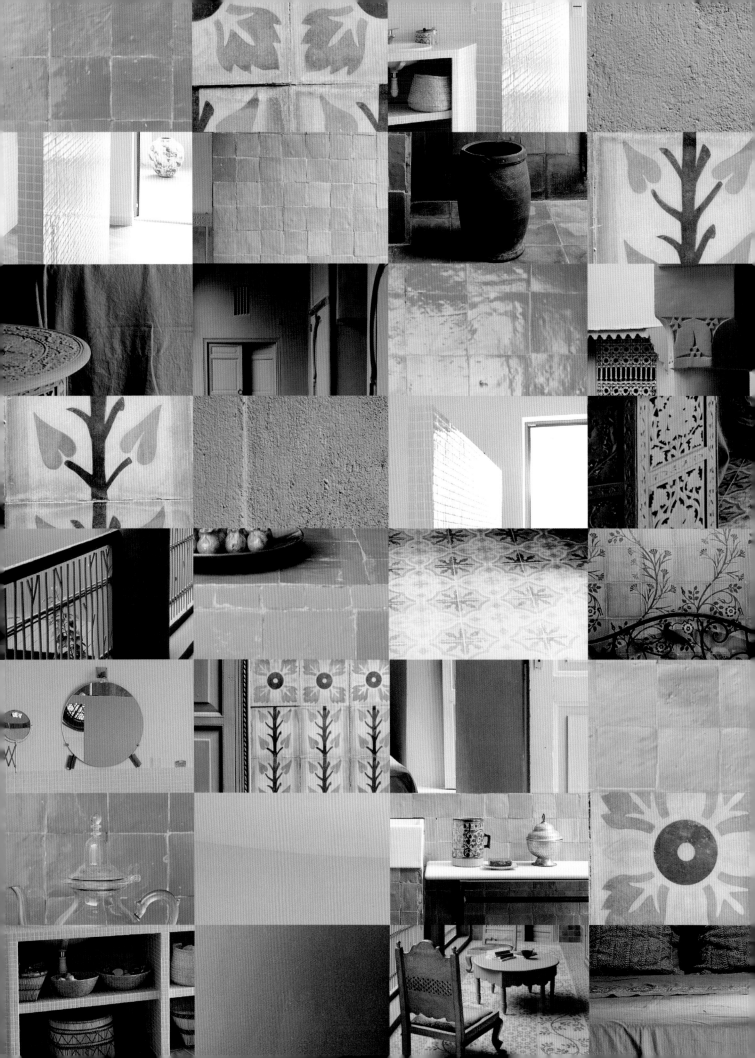

opalescence

pearlescence

sparkle

seascapes

WATERCOLOR

silk

TECHNIQUE

glass

reflective

indigo

The transparent and ever-changing nature of water makes it difficult to describe in terms of color, but it is usually represented in combinations of blues and greens. These variations on a blue/green theme take us from the sparkling brilliance of a Caribbean sea to the almost pea-green tones of a shaded pond, with stormy seas, swimming pools, and gently flowing rivers somewhere in between. Water can be stimulating but also soothing, and the same effects can be achieved in interiors. A bright turquoise in the bathroom will wake you up in the morning and soft blues and greens in a bedroom will lull you to sleep at night. Sometimes it is difficult to decide whether a color is blue or green, and, just as the sea changes color according to the sky, these water-related colors can change from blue to green depending on the light and the surroundings.

The reflective nature of water suggests colors that are not solid but have depth, qualities that are replicated in reflective surfaces such as tiles. Like water, blues and greens can be made to sparkle, especially when used with shiny metal and glass, which is why they work so well in kitchens and bathrooms. In other situations, the tendency for blues and greens to recede means that they can melt into the background, and for that reason they are also restful colors. However, they also have a reputation for being chilly, and unless used carefully, these colors can be oppressive and dull— though the right shade in the right place can also be surprisingly warm. Many of the pigments used in the creation of blue and green paints and dyes are derived from plants and the earth, and these dry, as opposed to wet, colors have a warmer, more comforting nature, especially when used with other earth colors, or as a foil to some of the more elusive watery tones.

Opposite: *The slightly uneven shape, texture, and glazed surface of these handmade tiles creates a rippling, watery effect, which makes them a perfect and practical choice for this style of bathroom.*

Reflective Mood

In a landscape, the colors associated with water and the sea are difficult to define because any apparent color is mostly a reflection of the sky. Consequently, the colors are elusive and continually changing according to the light as well as any movement on the surface. The essence of these colors are cool blues and greens and they can be used to create an atmosphere as varied as the landscape itself—often cool and calm but sometimes brighter, more dramatic and stimulating. The watery connections make this color range an

Opposite: *Mosaic tiles give a more textured and less clinical feel in this generous-sized bathroom. By tiling the walls, storage area, floor, and shower screen, the room looks functional yet at the same time luxurious. The collection of baskets are the perfect foil to all the hard edges and surfaces.*

Right: *Who could fail to be energized and invigorated by the intense color and raw, rustic nature of these Moroccan tiles? Their beauty is enhanced by the fact that they are handmade, which means that no two are the same, and their uneven surfaces give the color more depth and character.*

obvious choice for bathrooms and kitchens, especially as they are also associated with freshness and cleanliness. It is in these rooms that you are most likely to use glazed ceramic tiles, which as well as being water-resistant, easy-to-clean, and functional have a reflective quality, which makes them a perfect medium for water colors. The choice of color and finish is wide, from the palest aqua to deep aquamarine and even brilliant turquoise, and you can choose the pristine simplicity of plain, smooth finishes or opt for the more characterful variations found in handmade tiles.

As bathrooms are normally small spaces, and used for only short periods of time, they provide an opportunity to try something more daring, expensive, or luxurious, and an all-over tiled room can be beautiful as well as functional. In both kitchens and bathrooms, tiles provide an opportunity for a different form of color, which can either coordinate with the fixtures and fittings or add a splash of color, such as in a backsplash, tiled counter, or floor.

The reflective surface of glazed tiles will reflect the light and other colors in a room, changing their character and color depending on how and where they are used. Shiny surfaces respond well to bright illumination necessary for makeup or shaving in a bathroom, or food preparation in a kitchen, but lower levels of lighting can also mellow them and create an atmosphere more suited to relaxing baths or kitchen dining.

The hard surfaces of tiles can make a room feel cold, but you can remedy this by using the warmer greener shades such as eau de Nil and deep turquoise and by using a warmer form of lighting. Wooden floors and accessories will also help take the chill off, as will brightly colored accessories. For a cool, sophisticated atmosphere, you can also increase the sparkle and freshness with glass, chrome, and lots of white.

Right: *Choosing mosaic instead of smooth, evenly glazed tiles gives a warmer and more interesting surface with greater variation and subtlety of color.*

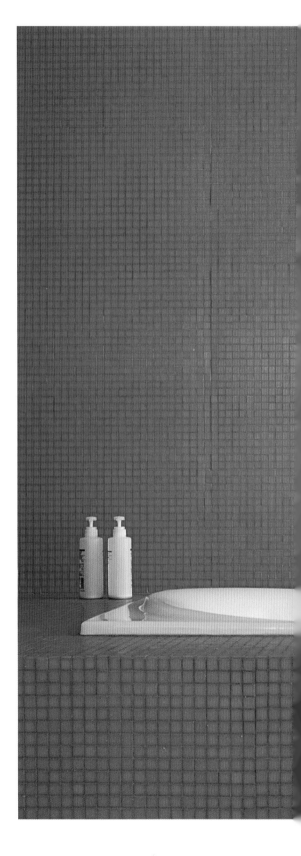

Restful Mood

Above: *These soft, subdued blue-greens are typical of the colors used on this style of architecture and furniture. Here they add to the feeling of welcome shade from the heat of the sun.*

Opposite: *The gentle colors in these beautiful, rustic tiles are perfectly complemented by the muted tones of the paint on the wall and door.*

Blues and greens based on earth dyes and pigments have a warmth and intensity that makes them restful. These soft, chalky, slightly smoky blues and greens, which are not too dark and not too bright, were much used in old houses, where, accompanied by the mellow tones of old polished wood, they created a tranquil atmosphere.

These are perfect colors for a simply furnished country cottage but also suit grander surroundings, where they look wonderful with red and blue Persian carpets and as a backdrop to ornate gilt-framed pictures and furniture, for example. They also help to create a peaceful ambience in a disciplined modern space and will have a calming influence on livelier, more colorful, and eclectic interiors. These restful colors are widely used in hot climates, where they appear to cool the heat of the sun and blend beautifully with the hotter, earthy colors of the landscape as well as with the traditional architecture, fabrics, and artefacts.

Muted blues and greens work best if they are given some air, so keep furnishings to a minimum and clutter at bay. Shades are preferable to drapes, and, as in hot countries, a restful atmosphere is achieved using lighter forms of furniture such as rattan and wooden-framed chairs and loungers rather than heavy upholstery. Blue becomes gray at night, so in a cooler climate, you may want to add other colors for evening warmth.

PEACEFUL COEXISTENCE

A color scheme made up entirely of blues and greens may be restful, but if monochrome is too monotonous, you may want to enlist other colors to help keep the peace.

● **Earth colors**
The earthy tones of browns, ochers, and burnt orange, whether in the form of wooden furniture and floors or rugs and textiles, will help to counteract any chilly tendencies of blues and greens.

● **Reds**
Red is often used with blue in rich patterns such as those found in old carpets and rugs, items that add color and richness without too much contrast to a blue or green environment.

● **Pinks**
From deep coral to the palest rose, pinks add warmth and a little femininity, if required. Use pinks for cushions and throws in soft textures such as silk, velvet, and cashmere, or as rugs and mats in chunky cotton or wool weaves.

● **Blues and greens**
Lighten the mood with touches of cleaner blues and greens, such as ice blue and pale lime green, in crisp cotton and linen or glazed tiles.

● **Black**
Furniture and accessories in black laquer, stained wood, or metal stand out beautifully against blue, especially if they are ornate items in wrought iron and carved wood.

MAKE IT WORK FOR YOU

Restful Mood

The style of architecture and furnishing suggests that this room has been designed to offer welcome respite from hot sunny days and balmy nights. The soft, restful colors and absence of clutter create an ambience guaranteed to induce a good night's sleep. Indeed, the overall atmosphere is one of quiet restraint, despite the ornate furniture and patterned floor. This is because the colors, typical of this ethnic style, although quite strong, are similar in tone and are carried throughout, on the walls, paintwork, fabrics, floor, and furniture. The various strengths of blue-green shades are emphasized by the lighting as well as the matte texture of the walls and the reflective surface of the tiled floor. The bedcover, table, and paintwork on the door are probably very similar in tone, but the light and surface textures make them look slightly different.

Not everyone has the luxury of space for a clutter-free bedroom but if you don't have a convenient alcove for your bed, you could create a peaceful spot within a busy room by curtaining off the bed, or a section of the room, using a translucent, colored muslin.

Opposite: The restricted color palette, plus plain walls, sparse furnishings, and tiled floor bring a peaceful, cell-like simplicity to this bedroom.

COLOR PALETTE

Gray blue
This color works well with other blue-green shades as they are similar to those found in verdigris, which is characterized by variety of tone rather than purity and uniformity of color.

Blue
A stronger, cleaner blue, which is purer in tone and somehow manages to look warm and cool at the same time. This bright blue will add definition and freshness to a collection of more muted tones.

Blue-green
In certain situations, this type of color definitely looks green, but with different lighting and combined with other colors, it can take on quite a blue appearance.

Indigo
Indigo is a plant dye, which is softer, warmer, and more subtle than other, harsher, purer blues. Like denim, this is a color that looks even better as it ages and fades.

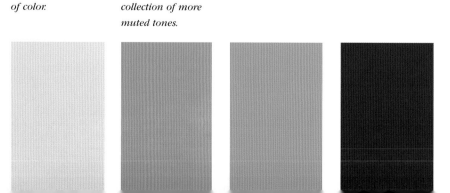

ADDED INGREDIENTS

Furniture
This ornate style of furniture is easy to find and often inexpensive, but to keep the sense of calm, limit it to one or two pieces. Too many patterned fabrics can look busy: introduce pattern in the form of decorative ironwork on a small table, chair, or bedhead instead.

Tiles
For bare floors, tiles are a practical and attractive option. A floor is a good place to add pattern as it won't dominate or distract, especially if colors blend in.

Lighting
These soft colors prefer gentle to harsh lighting. A single source of light positioned above the bed can function as a reading lamp as well as offering general illumination.

Fabrics
Keep things simple with a plain bedcover and limit the pillow count to just two small embroidered cushions. The hanging behind the bed works well as it is delicate and pretty rather than rich and heavy.

Useful Addresses

FABRICS, PAINT, WOOD FINISHES, AND WALLPAPER

Coley & Son (Wallpapers) Ltd
Cole & Son Distributors
Lee Jofa Inc
201 Central Avenue South
Bethgate NY 11714
1-800-453-3563
www.Cole-and-son.com
Wallpaper and paint. Traditional and modern designs.

Cowtan & Tout
111 Eighth Avenue, Suite 930
New York, NY 10011
212-647-6900
www.cowtan.com
Classic American fabric designs. Also includes fabrics from Colefax and Fowler and Jane Churchill.

Designers Guild
800-303-5413
www.designersguildus.com
Fabric and wallpaper. Visit the website for details on showrooms in the US.

Dulux
www.dulux.com
Large range of products online, also available in paint stores throughout the US.

Farrow & Ball
1054 Yonge Street
Toronto
Ontario Canada
www.farrow-ball.com
Manufacturers of traditional papers, paints, and eco-friendly paints. Available in selected stores throughout the US.

Green Planet Paints
PO Box 13
Patagonia, AZ 85624
520-394-2571
www.greenplanetpaints.com
Suppliers of natural paint. Visit the website for products and locations of stores in the US.

Marston & Langinger
www.marston-and-langinger.com
Bespoke conservatories and garden rooms with a range of furniture, accessories, and paint. Visit the website for online store and more information.

Mod Green Pod
617-670-2000
www.modgreenpod.com
Organic fabrics and vinyl-free wallpapers. Visit the website for stockists in the US.

Morris and Co
USA Corporate Office
285 Grand Avenue
3 Patriot Centre
Englewood New Jersey 07631
1-800-894-6185
www.william-morris.co.uk
Fabrics and wallpapers based on the designs of William Morris.

Sanderson
www.sandersonfabrics.co.uk
Suppliers of fabrics, wallpaper and paint. Visit the website for stockists in the US.

Stark Wallcovering
979 Third Avenue, 10th Floor
New York, NY 10022-276
212-355-7186
www.starkwallcovering.com
Suppliers of modern wallpapaer and fabric designs, plus antique and decorative wallcoverings. Visit the website for nearest showrooms.

The Old-Fashioned Milk Paint Company
436 Main Street
Groton Massachusetts 01450
978-448-6336
www.milkpaint.com
Suppliers of milk paint—a natural, nontoxic, and enviromentally friendly paint. Available in 20 colors for interior walls, furniture, cabinets, etc. online

Tried and Wood Finishes
14 Prospect Street
Trumansburg, NY 14886
607-387-9280
www.triedandtruewoodfinish.com
Suppliers of environmentally safe wood finishes.

FLOORING

Bamboo Hardwoods
4100 4th Ave. South
Seattle, WA 98134
1-800-607-2414
www.bamboohardwoods.com
Selection of bamboo and hardwood floors. Visit the website for products.

Flooring USA
www.flooringusa.net
Suppliers of ceramic, vinyl, hardwood, and laminate floors.

Mohawk Flooring
www.mohawk-flooring.com
Hardwood and laminate flooring. Company is exploring ways to make products more sustainable. Visit the website for products and location of stores.

Natural Cork
800-404-2675
www.naturalcork.com
Suppliers of cork and bamboo flooring. Visit the website for products.

World Floor Covering Association
www.wfca.org
Visit the website to find your nearest floor store and also a floorcovering professional.

FURNITURE AND ACCESSORIES

Ashley Furniture
www.ashleyfurniture.com
Top-selling furniture brand in the US. Visit the website for products and locations of stores.

Ikea
www.ikea.com/us
A valuable source of inexpensive, well-designed kitchens, furniture, rugs, fabrics, bedlinen, kitchen, and bathroom accessories.

Stark Furniture
979 Third Avenue, 10th Floor
New York, NY 10022-1276
212-355-7186
www.starkfinefurniture.com
Suppliers of contemporary furniture for every room of the house including upholstered sofas and glass tables. Visit the website for more details and nearest showrooms.

The Home Depot
www.homedepot.com
Retail website everything you will need for the home. Visit the website for locations of stores across the US.

CARPETS AND RUGS

Flooring USA
www.flooringusa.net
Carpets for every room in the house.

Mohawk Flooring
1-800-266-4295
www.mohawk-flooring.com
Carpets and rugs. Visit the website for products and location of stores.

Rugs USA
House Accents
Rugs USA
106 E Jericho Tpke
Mineola, NY 11501
1-800-982-7210
www.rugsusa.com
Wide range of Persian rugs, oriental rugs, and braided rugs for every room in the house. Visit the website for products.

Darius Antique and Decorative Rugs
979 Third Avenue, 10th Floor
New York, NY 10022-1276
212 355 7186
www.dariusantiquerugs.com
Suppliers of antique and decorative rugs by Darius. Visit the website for more details.

MODERN FURNITURE, LIGHTING, AND ACCESSORIES

All Modern Furniture
www.allmodernfurniture.com
Best selection of modern furniture online. Visit the website for products.

B & B Italia
www.bebitalia.it
Contemporary modern furniture including sofas, chairs, and bed tables. Visit the website for products.

Boltz Steel
227 Highway 25 North
Greenbrier, AR 72058
877-804-7650
www.boltz.com
Solid steel CD and DVD racks, plus tables and seating. Visit the website for products.

Cassina
(Headquarters) 200 McKay Road
Huntington Station, NY 11746
631-423-4560
www.cassinausa.com
Premier Italian modern furniture collection, includes furniture from Phillippe Starck. Visit the website for stores.

Grand Lighting
580 Grand Ave
New Haven, CT 06511
800-922-1469
www.grandlight.com
All types of lighting for inside and oustide the home. Visit the website for products.

Lamps US
2134 W Beltline Highway
Madison, WI 53713
1-877-526-7247
www.lampsusa.com
Online store for all types of lighting for the home including energy-efficient lighting.

Modern Classics
www.modernclassics.com
Retail website for designer furniture from Artoli, Mies Van de Rohe, and Colleen Gray. Items include sofas, chairs, daybeds, and tables. Visit the website to request catalog.

TEMA
800-895-8362
www.tema-usa.com
Contemporary furniture from bookcases, bedroom furniture to living room furniture. Visit the website for products.

HOUSEHOLD
ACCESSORIES

Bloomingdales
Bloomingdales.com
P.O. Box 8215
Mason, OH 45040
1-866-593-2540
www.bloomingdales.com
Everything from mattresses, home decor, vases, candles, and kitchen equipment. Visit the website for locations of stores across the US.

Crate and Barrel
Customer Service Department
1860 West Jefferson Avenue
Naperville, IL 60540
800-967-6696
www.crateandbarrel.com
Suppliers of home furnishings and bedlinen. Visit the website for products and locations of stores across the US.

Designers Guild
800-303-5413
www.designersguildus.com
Bedlinen, cushions, throws, and fragrant candles for the home available online.

Dillard's
www.dillards.com
Home furnishings including table linen, bedding, china, and home decor. Visit the website for location of stores.

Home and Gifts
www.homeandgifts.biz
Online store with everything for your home from night lights to mirrors and vases.

Macys
1-800-289-6229
www.macys.com
Everything for the home including beds, kitchen equipment, and rugs. Visit the website for products and location of stores.

Saks
www.saksfifthavenue.com
Home accessories and furnishings. Visit the website for products and location of stores.

Sears, Roebuck & Co.
www.sears.com
Home accessories and furnishings for the home. Visit the website for products and location of stores.

Tomorrow's World
9647 First View Street
Norfolk, VA 23503
800-229-7571
www.tomorrowsworld.com
Organic mattresses, bedding, towels, and natural candles. Visit the website for products.

BATHROOM AND
KITCHEN FITTINGS

Armstrong
www.armstrong.com
Suppliers of kitchen and bathroom cabinets. available in different woods and styles. Also includes laminated cabinets. Visit the website for products, to request a catalog, and to find location of nearest store.

Caesar Stone
6840 Hayvenhurst Ave. Suite 100
Van Nuys, CA 91406
818-779-0999
www.caesarstoneus.com
Quartz surfaces and countertops for kitchens and bathrooms. Visit the website for products.

Grohe
241 Covington Drive
Bloomingdale, IL 60108
630-582-7711
www.groheamerica.com
Luxury bathroom and kitchen faucets and hand showers. Visit the website for products.

Kitchen Place
207-667-4439
www.kitchenplace.com
All wood designed custom-made kitchen and bathroom cabinets, plus built-in furniture. Visit the website for products.

Kohler
1-800-456-4537
www.kohler.com
A range of bathtubs, faucets, sinks, and showers. Visit the website for location of stores.

Wasauna
10450 N. 74th Street, Suite 130
Scottsdale, AZ 85258
888-846-0661
www.wasauna.com
Manufacturers of luxury bathrooms. Visit website for products and more information.

ANTIQUES AND OLD FURNITURE

Antique Collectibles Directory
www.antiquecollectiblestore.com
National antique and collectible directory plus a guide to flea markets and antique stores across the US. May have to become a member to enjoy the full benefits of site.

Olde Good Things
(National Store)
400 Gilligan Street
Scranton, Pennsylvania 18508
888-233-9678
www.oldegoodthings.com
Architectural antiques and artifacts. Visit the website for locations of stores in the US.

ARCHITECTURAL SALVAGE

Urban Archeology
www.urbanarcheology.com
Architectural salvage business.

TRADITIONAL AND ECOLOGICAL BUILDING AND DECORATING MATERIALS AND ADVICE

Green Building Supply
www.greenbuildingsupply.com
Suppliers of environmentally friendly cleaners, wood countertops, natural flooring, wool carpeting, and nontoxic building materials.

Healthy Building Network
www.healthybuilding.net
National network of green building professionals.

Healthy House Institute
www.healthyhouseinstitute.com
A web-based resource for environmental health and green building information.

Green Building Exchange
305 Main Street
Redwood City, CA 94063
650-369-4900
www.greenbuildingexchange.com
Provides information on sustainable building practices and green building professionals.

Green Building Resources Guide
www.thegreenguide.com
Database of green building materials and products. Visit the website for more details.

United States Green Building Council
1800 Massachusetts Avenue NW
Suite 300
Washington, DC 20036
800-795-1747
www.usgbc.org
Committed to expanding sustainable building practices. Online courses and information on green building.

INFORMATION ON THE CONSERVATION OF OLD PROPERTIES

Old House Journal Online
www.oldhousejournal.com
A website and bi-monthly magazine for everything old-house owners need to know about caring for, living in, and enjoying their old houses.

Historic House Colors
www.historichousecolors.com
Service available via email that assists homeowners and businesses in the selection of exterior colors. It is available for all types of historic homes as well as new constructions.

Preservation Web
www.preservationweb.com
The definitive guide to historic preservation services and products. Find a historic preservation architect and other specialized services.

Index

Page numbers in italics refer Page numbers in italics refer to captions.

a

achromatic colors 13
amber 118
amethyst 62, *62*, 118
Asian style 122, *122*

b

bamboo 133
bathrooms
    blue and green 148
    dark colors 16, 50, *52*
    dramatic colors *73*, 74, 78, *93*
    electric colors 83
    white 30, 35
bedrooms
    dramatic colors 78
    pattern in *110*, 110–11
    white accessories 35, *35*
    white plus red 40
beige 73, 115
black 19, *46*, 52, 78, 151
blue 19, 48
    cobalt blue 94
    in color palettes *80*, 96
    historic paint ranges 90, 94
    Klein blue 48
    Prussian blue 90
    related colors 74
    with green 144–53
    with red 73, 151
    with white 48, *48*
blue-green 44, *150*
bright colors 68–85
    with white 38, 73
brown 52, *62*, 115, *115*, 151

c

carmine 94
carpets and rugs 16, 42, 98, 112, 117
    dark 54
    Oriental 42, 98, 112, 117, 121
    white 35
ceiling roses 16
chandeliers 112, 121, 139
Chinese style 122

choosing colors 20–3
collections, displaying 61, 111
color palettes
    disciplined *9*, *58*, 58–63, *60*, *109*
    historical colors 96–7
    jewel colors 120–1
    restful colors 152–3
    vivid colors 80–1
    white plus green plus red 46–7
    white plus pink 62–3
color-wash technique 100
color wheel 12
cool colors 12, 14
cornices 97
cushions 42, 73

d

dados 110, 131
dark colors
    drapes and shades 50, 54
    floors 40, 46, 47, 50, 52, 54
    with white *38*, *50*, 50–4, *52*
denim 48
disciplined schemes *9*, *58*, 58–63, *60*, *109*
distemper 93
distressed interiors *98*, 98–100
distressing techniques
    furniture 134
    walls 100
drapes and shades 117
    dark colors 50, 54
    shadow effects 16

e

eggshell paint 93
electric colors 82–4

f

floors
    dark *40*, 46, 47, 50, *52*, 54
    liming technique 134
    natural-fiber coverings 56, 133
    in older properties 98, 134
    painted 28, 30, 73, 134
    tiles 30, 137
    white 28, 30, *30*
    wood 56
    see also carpets and rugs

furniture, painted 60, 73, 131
    distressing technique 134

g

glass 30
glazes (paint technique) 100
gloss paint 16, 93, 137
gold 19, *88*, 120
granite 52, 132
green *18*, 19, 44
    in color palettes *46*, *80*, *96*, *120*, *138*
    emerald 118, *120*
    forest green 44, 94
    historic color ranges 94
    jade 118
    lime green 44, 46, *62*
    olive green 44
    pea green 94
    related colors 74
    with blue 144–53
    with white 44–5
    with white and red 46, 46–7
gray *16*, 52, 73, 98, *140*, 140
greige 115

h

historic colors/paint ranges 88, 90, *90*, *93*, 94, 102
    finishes 92–3
    light-absorbing properties 15
    in modern houses 102–3
    white 26, 32, 136
hues 13

j

jewel color schemes *118*, 118–21, *120*

k

khaki *138*
kilims 42, 98, 112, 117
kitchens
    blue and green 148
    dark colors 50
    dramatic schemes 78, *79*
    electric colors 83
    green 44

white 30, 35, 50
white with green and red 46,
  46–7
white with pale colors 56
white with red 40, 40

l

latex paint 93
lavender 48
light direction 15
lighting 84, 84, 139
    chandeliers 112, 121, 139
    wall lights 84, 139
limestone, polished 137
liming technique 134
linoleum 133

m

Matisse, Henri 20, 71
medieval colors 112
Mediterranean colors 16, 48, 94
metal 30, 54
mirrors 30, 56, 121
Modernism 60, 90, 94
moldings, decorative 16, 97
monochromatic schemes 13, 128–9,
  129

n

natural materials 132, 132–3
north/northeast-facing rooms 15

o

off-white 138
older properties 71, 77, 88, 98–100,
  134–5, 135
    see also historic colors/paint
    ranges
open-plan interiors 84
orange 19, 45, 151
Oriental carpets 42, 98, 112, 117, 121

p

paintings
    displaying 61

as inspiration 20, 20, 58, 61, 68,
  112
pale colors 126–41
Palladian colors 90
paneling 38, 52, 96, 97
pastel colors 131, 131
pattern 73, 106 13, 117
pink 19, 45, 80, 103, 151
    in color palettes 62, 80, 96, 110
    historic paint ranges 90
    in older interiors 98
    shocking pink 9, 45, 64–5, 65
    with white 62, 62
primary colors 12, 71–7
psychology of color 18, 18–19
purple 19, 118

r

red 18, 19, 74, 118
    accessories 42, 42
    in color palettes 46, 110
    historic paint ranges 90, 94
    related colors 74
    ruby 118, 120
    with blue 73, 151
    with white 40, 73
    with white and green 46, 46–7
rubber flooring 133

s

seagrass floor coverings 56, 98, 133
seasons 15
"shabby chic" 134–5, 135
shades 13, 71
shadows, effects of 16
silver 19
sisal floor coverings 56, 98, 133
size of rooms, color and 14
slate 52, 132
souk style 112
south/southwest-facing rooms 15
stainless steel 30, 47
stencils 131
stone 52, 132, 132, 133

t

taupe 115
terra-cotta 16
tiles 30, 137, 144, 147, 148, 148, 150

floors 30, 137
    stone 52, 133
times of day 14
tints 13, 71
tones 13, 71
topaz 118
trompe l'oeil paint effects 100, 126
trying out colors 14, 20
turquoise 110, 118

v

vermilion 94

w

wall lights 84, 139
wallpaper 54, 56, 73, 117, 121
warm colors 12, 14
white 19, 26, 26–35, 46
    accessories 35, 35, 98, 136
    all-white schemes 28–9, 29, 60
    brilliant white 26, 32
    carpets and rugs 35
    floors 28, 30, 30
    historic paint ranges 26, 32
    and light direction 15
    and the seasons 15
    shiny surfaces 30
    warming up 32, 32–3
white plus color 38–65
    blue 48, 48
    dark colors 38, 50, 50–4, 52
    green 44–5
    green and red 46, 46–7
    pink 62, 62
    red 40, 73
    subtle contrasts 56, 56
wood, natural 52, 56, 133
woodwork, painting 77, 93
wool 132, 133

y

yellow 19, 74
    chrome yellow 90, 94
    historic paint ranges 90, 94
    related colors 74
    yellow ocher 90, 94

Picture Credits

Note: unless otherwise specified, all pictures used on page 2 and on chapter openers feature elsewhere in the book.

4 Jérôme Galland/Daniel Rozensztroch, Caroline Tiné; **5** Jérôme Galland/Marie Kalt; **6–7** Kaido Haagen; **8** Mai-Linh/Catherine Ardouin/Lighting artist: Matteo Messervy; **13** Vincent Leroux/Catherine Ardouin; **15** Vincent Leroux/Christine Puech; **16** Didier Gaillard/Catherine Hornez; **17** Michel Bousquet; **18** Vincent Leroux/Gaël Reyre, Daniel Rozensztroch; **21** Philippe Garcia/Catherine Ardouin; **22–3** Vincent Leroux/Catherine Ardouin; **27** Charlotte Louppe; **28–9** Bertrand Limbour/Catherine Ardouin; **30–1** Mai-Linh/Catherine Ardouin; **32** José Van Riele/Daniel Rozensztroch; **33** Alexis Armanet/Interior architect: Emmanuel Renoird; **34** Mai-Linh/Catherine Ardouin; **35** José Van Riele/Daniel Rozensztroch; **39** Mai-Linh/Catherine Ardouin; **40** Mai-Linh/Architect: Anne Geistdoerfer, Double G agency; **41** Emmanuel Barbe/Gaël Reyre; **42** Jérôme Galland/Marie Kalt; **43** David Souffan/Interior architect: Emmanuel Renoird; **44–5** Marie-José Jarry/Catherine Ardouin; **47** Olivier Amsellem/David Souffan; **49 top** Marie-Pierre Morel; **bottom** Marie-Pierre Morel/Daniel Rozensztroch; **50–1** Emmanuel Barbe/Catherine Ardouin, Marie Kalt/Architect: Johanna Grawunder; **52** Olivier Amsellem/David Souffan; **53** Eric Flogny/Marion Bayle, Christine Puech; **54 top** Jacques Giaume; **bottom** Alexandre Weinberger/Catherine Ardouin; **55** Emmanuel Barbe/Catherine Ardouin, Marie Kalt/Architect: Johanna Grawunder; **56** Jérôme Galland/Daniel Rozensztroch, Caroline Tiné; **57** Annabel Elston/Marie Kalt; **59** Philippe Garcia/Catherine Ardouin; **60 top** Vincent Leroux/Philippe Deleau, David Souffan; **bottom** Christophe Dugied/Christine Puech; **61** Pénéloppe Chauvelot/Michelle Bocquillon; **63** Vincent Leroux/Catherine Ardouin; **64 bottom left** Olivier Amsellem/David Souffan; **64–5** Marie-José Jarry/Catherine Ardouin; **66 column 1, row 5** Mai-Linh/Catherine Ardouin, Réka Magyar **69** Mai-Linh/Catherine Ardouin/Lighting artist: Matteo Messervy; **70** Marie-Pierre Morel/Catherine Ardouin; **71** Philippe Garcia/Catherine Ardouin; **72** Nicolas Tosi/Catherine Ardouin; **73** Emmanuel Barbe/Catherine Ardouin; **75** Vincent Leroux/Christine Puech/Brand creator, Mia Zia: Valerie Barkowski; **76** Vincent Leroux/Catherine Ardouin; **77** Philippe Garcia/Catherine Ardouin; **79** Eric Flogny/Daniel Rozensztroch/Damsgard Country Mansion, tel: +47 559 40 870; **81** Vincent Leroux/Catherine Ardouin; **82** Olivier Amsellem/David Souffan; **83** Michel Bousquet/Caroline Blum; **84/85** Emmanuel Barbe/Catherine Ardouin; **88–9** Jérôme Galland/Marie Kalt; **90** Christophe Dugied/Pauline Ricard-André; **91** Jérôme Galland/Adelaïde Nicotra's house; **92** Eric Flogny/Daniel Rozensztroch/Damsgard Country Mansion, tel: +47 559 40 870; 93 Vincent Leroux/Catherine Ardouin, Sylvia Marius; **94** Jérôme Galland/Adelaïde Nicotra's house; **95** Philippe Garcia/Marie Kalt, Christine Puech; **97** Jérôme Galland/Marie Kalt; **99** Philippe Garcia/Catherine Ardouin; **100** Philippe Garcia/Catherine Ardouin/Architects: Rosella and Roberto Baciocchi; **101** Philippe Garcia/Christine Puech/Photographer: Pascal Bennett; **102** Marie-Pierre Morel/Furniture designer: Christophe Delcourt; **103** Vincent Leroux/Christine Puech/House to rent in Marrakech, tel: +33 1 42 77 03 71; **106–7** Francis Kompalitch/Catherine Hornez; **108/109** Christophe Valentin; **111** Philippe Garcia/Sylvia Marius; **112** Paul Lepreux/Marie Kalt; **113** Philippe Garcia/J-Pascal Billaud; **114** Vincent Leroux/Christine Puech/Stylist: Agnès Emery; **116** Vincent Leroux/Catherine Ardouin; **117** Eric Flogny/Daniel Rozensztroch; **118** Eric Flogny/Daniel Rozensztroch/Damsgard Country Mansion, tel: +47 559 40 870; **119** Vincent Leroux/Christine Puech; **121** Philippe Garcia/Catherine Ardouin/Global designer: Stephane Plassier; **122** Dan Tobin Smith/David Souffan; **123** Vincent Leroux/Christine Puech, David Souffan; **127** Vincent Leroux/Catherine Ardouin/Philippe Guilmin; **128 top:** Marie-Pierre Morel/Gérald Le Signe, Catherine Ardouin; **bottom:** Christophe Dugied/Pauline Ricard-André; **129** Christophe Dugied/Pauline Ricard-André; **130** Gilles de Chabaneix/Catherine de Chabaneix; **132** Gilles de Chabaneix/Catherine Ardouin/Jacqueline Morabito house; **133** Jacques Caillaut/Isabelle Laforge; **134** Nicolas Tosi/Catherine Ardouin; **135 top** Francis Kompalitch/Catherine Hornez; **bottom** Vincent Leroux/Catherine Ardouin/Philippe Guilmin's guest house, Brussels; **136–7** Alexis Armanet/David Souffan; **139** Annabel Elston/Marie Kalt; **140** Francis Amiand; **141** Nicolas Tosi/Julie Borgeaud; **145** Vincent Leroux/Christine Puech/Stylist and owner: Agnès Emery; **146** Louis Gaillard/Catherine Hornez; **147** Vincent Leroux, Christine Puech/Stylist and owner: Agnès Emery; **148–9** Vincent Leroux/Catherine Ardouin; **150** Vincent Leroux, Christine Puech/Stylist and owner: Agnès Emery; **151** Vincent Leroux, Christine Puech/Stylist and owner: Agnès Emery; **153** Vincent Leroux, Christine Puech/Stylist and owner: Agnès Emery; **160** Mai-Linh/CatherineArdouin.